D1719785

NARRATIVE FISSURES

NARRATIVE FISSURES

Reading and Rhetoric

Nita Schechet

Madison • Teaneck
Fairleigh Dickinson University Press

Associated University Presses
2010 Eastpark Boulevard
Cranbury, NJ 08512

The paper used in this publication meets the requirements of the American National Standard for Permanence of Paper for Printed Library Materials Z39.48-1984.

Library of Congress Cataloging-in-Publication Data

Schechet, Nita, 1952–
    Narrative fissures : reading and rhetoric / Nita Schechet.
        p.   cm.
    Includes bibliographical references and index.
    ISBN 0-8386-4057-5 (alk. paper)
    1. English fiction—History and criticism—Theory, etc.   2. American fiction—History and criticism—Theory, etc.   3. Books and reading—English-speaking countries.   4. English language—Rhetoric.   5. Narration (Rhetoric)   I. Title.
PR826.S34   2005
823.009—dc22   2004016350

Contents

Acknowledgments

"Words pay no debts."
—Shakespeare, *Troilus and Cressida*

Pandarus may be right, but what can never be paid can at least be acknowledged. I will be brief—and partial:

To Rachel Back, poet, scholar, beloved friend, without whom there would be no book, and little else;

To Rivka and Ilan Ankava, dearest of friends, who make everything possible, and to Izzy Ankava, greatest of gifts;

To Ruth Nevo and Elizabeth Freund, cherished friends and teachers;

To my loving long-distance enthusiasts, my father, Hy Schechet, and friend, Martha Venditti Schechet;

To Mildred and Ian Karten, so giving to so many;

To Drs. Ronnie Ban, Oded Olsha, Mercedes Riembau, Bella Kaufman, and Nathan Cherny, with more thanks than words;

To the vibrant and inspiring graduate students of my Lafer Center workshop on rhetorical criticism and feminist methodology, and to Tamar El-Or who opened that door; to Christine Retz and Harry Keyishian at AUP, who led this book to press with attentive grace;

And to those whom I haven't thanked by name but to whom I owe much, I hope you know who you are. I know I do. I am grateful and indebted to you all.

Finally, this book is given in bereft dedication to my sister Ellen, whose lost life is an ever-present absence in my own.

Permission for the use of quoted material is gratefully acknowledged, as follows:

"A Woman Sings a Song for a Soldier Come Home," from THE COLLECTED POEMS OF WALLACE STEVENS by Wallace Stevens, copyright 1954 by Wallace Stevens and renewed 1982 by Holly Stevens. Used by permission of Alfred A. Knopf, a division of Random House, Inc. and Faber and Faber Ltd.

"Myth" by Muriel Rukeyser, reprinted by permission of William L. Rukeyser.

NARRATIVE FISSURES

.

Introduction: Textual Fissures

> The necessary thing . . . is to enlarge the possibility of intelligible discourse between people quite different from one another in interest, outlook, wealth, and power, and yet contained in a world where, tumbled as they are into endless connection, it is increasingly difficult to get out of each other's way.
>
> —Clifford Geertz (1988: 147)

THE INTERDISCIPLINARY NEXUS OF NARRATIVE, THE FOCUS OF THIS book, is currently emerging as that "necessary thing" facilitating intelligible intersubjective discourse within and across contemporary academic and human-service professions. Cultural studies, ethnography, psychotherapy, historiography, critical legal studies, education, communication, and medicine are among the diverse fields that share an interest in the epistemological potential of narrative understanding, creating a need for professionally reflectively reflexive readers and writers that was once exclusively in the literary domain. The rhetorical concerns of both reading and writing narrative presented in this book derive from the field of narratology[1] (originating in literature) and discourse analysis[2] (originating in linguistics)—rhetorical concerns that are now spreading through and across disciplines.[3] The challenge—and one of the joys—of working with narrative across disciplines is the openness of the field. It is well worth overcoming the inevitable agoraphobia.

In aspiration, this is a how-to book—suggestive, not prescriptive—for advanced students in diverse fields, aiming to proffer a toolbox for reading and writing that is epistemologically shared though not subject-specific. My choice of fissure as metaphor for sites of textual entry is intended to keep in view the physicality of textuality.[4] This perspective shares Michael Calvin McGee's understanding of texts as fashioned from what he terms "fragments," containing text and context while marking the essential incompleteness of our critical focus (1999: 73). McGee's working instructions are relevant here. He directs textual critics to

11

[m]ake it clear that [the text] is a *fragment*. Look for the particular locu-
tions that implicate its sources. Show where cultural conventions are
presupposed. Locate the places where [the text] is trying to create, or is
seeking, its audience. . . . Frequently the best evidence you have of the
missing parts of a text are there in front of you as implications of the
fragment you are looking at. Certainly, every fragment is a map of the
structures that will make it complete, and in that sense focus on a part
can be a speculative, "incomplete" study of the whole.

Bringing textual fissuring into view in the reading and writing processes, in ways that this book demonstrates, offers a methodology to
accomplish this mapping.[5]

McGee finds a role reversal among writers/speakers and readers/
audiences in contemporary culture, where "text construction is
now something done more by the consumers than by the producers
of discourse" (1999: 76). My sense of this moment is not of role
reversal but of a boundary-challenging intimacy. Applying the concept of fissures to reading and writing narrative, the substance of
this book, illustrates this intimacy, conceptualized by Celeste Michelle Condit in agonistic terms (1999: 496).[6] Put differently, fissures function similarly to that which Wolfgang Iser has
conceptualized as textual "blanks," "the switch that activates the
reader into using his own ideas in order to fulfill the intention of
the text" (1989: 28). Iser's blanks are writer-initiated; fissures are
either writer-initiated or reader-sought. The critical reader must be
critically aware of being activated. I conceive of this book as a collection of exercises aimed at enhancing that critical awareness, to
be applied by each reader in developing reflectively reflexive reading and writing skills according to personal and professional needs.[7]
"Reflection" is a term popular in many professions these days, yet
it often remains inarticulate, even solipsistic. Rhetorical analyses[8]
such as those I demonstrate throughout this book anchor the
vaguely formulated intuitive reflections of the professional in a systematic and clearly articulated textual foundation.[9]

Potential texts are, of course, everywhere. Our textbook is the
world around us, and examples are as available as our attention to
them permits.[10] To demonstrate my concept of fissures as openings
into textual intentionality ("what the text <u>does</u>, rather than what
the text is meant to mean" [Iser 1993: 6]), I begin with short textual
units, the substance of this introductory chapter, asking its purport

of each stylistic choice. The rest of this book will then apply this concept to the longer textual units of narrative.

To begin with a richly provocative text, I borrow two quotations from a study of gender aspects of changes in the culture of political protest in Israel.[11] Sara Helman and Tamar Rapoport (1997) interpret the Israeli peace movement's Women in Black as signaling a profound change in Israel's protest culture. Women in Black is an informal, female-initiated grassroots movement against the Israeli occupation of territories conquered in Israel's 1967 war with its Arab neighbors. This movement began during the first Palestinian Intifada (1988) and continued until the Oslo peace treaties seemed to be on their way to implementation (1994), and has been revived in response to their failure and the consequent continuing occupation. Every Friday afternoon women dressed in black gather for an hour at a central Jerusalem juncture, carrying signs calling for an end to the occupation. Women come as they can, and numbers vary with the meteorological and political climates. Positioned prominently on a traffic isle at a busy time of day, the women are exposed to a great deal of verbal abuse, much of it from taxi drivers passing by or stopped at the adjacent light. As part of their study, Helman and Rapoport had their male research assistants interview these taxi drivers about their views of Women in Black. Here is my translation from the Hebrew of the comments of two of these men (pp. 185–86):

These women, when they're standing, their shitty puss already gets on your nerves. Those four-eyed women with their glasses, all of them Ashkenazi [Jews of European origin] . . . I work with them, I know what this is. I know that style. They don't believe in religion. If they had a drop of religion, like the [Jews of North African and Middle-Eastern origin], they wouldn't be protesting. They don't believe in religion, they are hurting the state, they are hurting Israel. These are women who are bored, without husbands, without anything in their lives, they have nothing to do and they are looking for attention.

These are the type of people who didn't live in the State of Israel before it was founded. These are people who don't know the real problem of Israel, of the wars of the Israeli nation—in my opinion, they are people who came from Europe. They came to this country when the country already existed, when the dirty work was already done. First of all they are all white, Ashkenazi. I think also that these women are middle-class or more. Sitting well . . . having everything. . . . Their [willingness to give up territory] comes, in my opinion, from lack of knowledge of the real problem of the Israeli nation. . . . We're talking about a type of person that doesn't know the real problem of the Israeli nation.

What can we learn about the speakers' worldviews from these lines? The fissures inviting entry are several. Through repetition and lexical choices we glimpse both speakers' epistemology and find a similar experiential base. The first speaker claims to know his subjects well through working with them (repeated three times with slight variation); his claim to authority is experience-based. The second speaker asserts the absence of experience-derived knowledge on the part of the women protesters. The women were not in Israel before the founding of the state; therefore, they cannot know "the real problem" of Israel (repeated three times). Note the second speaker's use of the definite article ("the") and the correspondingly confident "real" (and of course the assertion of a single problem facing the state). Both speakers offer an epistemology interestingly contrasting that of the "bespectacled" women they discuss, whose knowledge, as they dismissively suggest by this image, derives from books. This is an epistemology dominant in oral cultures, which are characterized by learning by

apprenticeship, . . . by discipleship . . . , by listening, by repeating what they hear, by mastering proverbs and ways of combining and recombining them, by assimilating other formulary materials, by participation in a kind of corporate retrospection—not by study in the strict sense. (Ong 1982: 9)

Similarly, we see a worldview shaped by binary oppositions, both in the lines quoted above and even more extensively in the fuller original text, a divide between Jews West and East, religious and secular, academic and not. Summarizing and totalizing the Ashkenazi and "white" origin they claim as common to "all" the women protesters, the speakers reveal a world split in two, these binary oppositions shaping this worldview and the experiential epistemology from which it draws its authority.

Another interesting fissure inviting interpretive entry evident in the first speaker's speech is the rhetorically effective universalization. His assertion that "their shitty puss already gets on your nerves" (even before "you" have read their placards and banners) articulates the assumption that the speaker's personal distaste is shared, conflating personal and communal opinion. The speaker both avoids assuming responsibility for his opinion and implicates his listener. Active intervention—and dissent—on the part of the listener is needed to counter the assumed universality of the assertion implied by the second-person "your." The silent listener, politely not interrupting, and most certainly the male graduate student interviewing this taxi driver, is not likely to dissent. Universalization creates the effect of assent and/or complicity, deriving its power from conventions of conversation which discourage interruption of speaker by listener. (A similar strategy of universalization might partially explain the extraordinary rhetorical success of former U.S. president Ronald Reagan. For example, in a 1982 press conference on returning from Latin America, Reagan said: "Well, I learned a lot when I went down there to find out from them their views. You'd be surprised. They're all individual countries." The turn to the second-person [*You'd be surprised*] perhaps distracts the listener from the unsettling comprehension that the president of the United States is asserting his discovery of a geographical fact— that Latin America is comprised of many different countries—that any elementary school pupil should be expected to know.)

Tracking the fissures in the remarks of these two taxi drivers (repetition, lexical selection, universalization) reveals much about the speakers of these brief texts: an experiential epistemology, a binary worldview, a universalist rhetorical strategy. These insights can instruct the attentive listener and, wisely applied, help shape a rhetorically successful (that is, persuasive) response. For example, an experiential epistemology would not respond well to the suggestion that researching "the real problem" of the state of Israel could teach anything worthwhile. The speaker believes in the value of experience, not libraries. Any approach on the epistemological level should accord with—or at least proceed from—the speaker's, creating a new experience that can provide grounds for reassessment. His binary worldview could possibly be challenged by introduction to protesters who are religious, or Jews of Eastern origin, whose absence is axiomatic for the speaker. Worlds divided into two may open to revision in encountering realities not accommodated by binarism. Even the insights consequent on analysis of the speaker's universalization of his response to the physical appearance of the

women protesters can be used in formulating effective responses.
(And in fact, in this study they were anticipated, hence the selection of male graduate students to interview the taxi drivers.) Pursuing these fissures through to insights about the speaker's
construction of the world can greatly enrich professionals engaged
in interpersonal communication across and between disciplines.

Figurative language (metaphor, simile, metonymy, synecdoche)
can also function as fissures offering hermeneutic gifts. Take, for
example, the cliche: "You can bring a horse to water but you can't
make it drink." The accepted meaning of this extended metaphor
is benign, generous even: one cannot force someone to do something, one can only show the way. However, closer analysis of this
metaphor reveals an interestingly supercilious subtext. Metaphors
are comparisons, and this one compares its implied student to a
beast; the teacher or guide knows where the truth/knowledge
(water) is, and can at best lead the beast to it. In other words, this
extended metaphor, flattering to speaker and listener both, holds
its object in extremely low regard. While ostensibly generous, es-
chewing force, it is concomitantly brutally damning, reinforcing hierarchical power relations, a subtext made visible by closely reading
the components of the extended metaphor and the comparisons
they imply. There are several ways to say "we can't force anyone to
do anything"; one can learn something about a speaker who
chooses this cliche over other available options. Of course selection
does not imply conscious intention on the part of the speaker. The
question is not "what did the speaker mean by what s/he said";
rather, we are asking the meaning, always in context, of salient stylistic features.

The choice of idioms can also provide fissured sites of hermeneutic entry. To illustrate this point, I have chosen an extract from
the television guide of the English-language edition of the Hebrew
daily newspaper *Ha'aretz* (4 April 1999) that describes a film as
being "about a young girl who gets herself pregnant." The idiom
"gets herself pregnant" cannot literally be true; pregnancy is not
achieved singly. The expression describes an unmarried expectant
mother, and contains an element of blame: It is the woman's fault;
she did it herself. This film description, written in the spring of
1999, perpetuates that worldview by continuing to use this idiom
for single motherhood. That is the effect of selection of this idiom
in this context. Again, the issue here is obviously not the intention

of the speaker. The *Ha'aretz* writer and the horse-leading teacher would probably not recognize themselves in my analysis of their words. Intentionality is irrelevant to such analysis, and rhetorical criticism (Foss 1996) does not include intentionality in its scope. The question asked of any text is how it is understood by its reader; in terms of speech act theory, its illocutionary effect (Searle 1968: 47).

Analysis of illocutionary effect ranges from the single word through the sentence to the narrative whole. Parts of speech can reveal point of view; even seemingly objective nouns can reveal latent ideologies. A "Calvin and Hobbes" cartoon that turns on the noun "zoo" eloquently demonstrates this. Young Calvin tells his cat (Hobbes) that his mother would like to know if they want to go to the zoo that day. Hobbes asks if they can tour a prison afterward, prompting Calvin to respond to his mother "no thanks." A zoo, from the viewpoint of Calvin's mother, is a leisure-time activity; from the perspective of Calvin's pet cat, it is a jail. Learning to recognize the point of view implied even in seemingly objective nouns gives access to other perspectives.

So too the myth of the "unmarked" pronoun. As MacKay and Fulkerson show, the falseness of the apparent universality of the masculine in a sentence like "A lawyer must frequently argue his case out of court" is exposed when subjects are asked to determine whether such a sentence refers both to women and men, only to women, or only to men (1979: 661–71). While most respondents answered "correctly" (as taught in schoolbook grammar), the reaction times of male and female respondents to sentences like this one varied significantly, with female respondents taking longer to reach the "correct" answer (that the sentence applies equally to males and to females). Feminist linguistic research has exposed the patriarchal bias of this supposedly neutral masculine form (de Beauvoir 1949; Silveira 1980; Greenberg 1966). Muriel Rukeyser, rewriting the story of Oedipus ("Myth," 1973), has given it poetic utterance:

> Long afterward, Oedipus, old and blinded, walked the
> roads.   He smelled a familiar smell.   It was
> the Sphinx.   Oedipus said, "I want to ask you one question.
> Why didn't I recognize my mother?"   "You gave the
> wrong answer," said the Sphinx.   "But that was what
> made everything possible," said Oedipus.   "No," she said.

> "When I asked, What walks on four legs in the morning,
> two at noon, and three in the evening, you answered,
> Man.   You didn't say anything about woman."
> "When you say Man," said Oedipus, "you include women
> too. Everyone knows that."   She said, "That's what
> you think."

Commonly held assumptions ("everyone knows that"), the less visible subtexts of our linguistic choices, often offer rich fissures for interpretive entry.

Another example of the interpretive potential of the taken-for-granted emerges in the following comment on the evening news made by an Israeli television viewer. His view is that "What they show speaks for itself. The news shows what happens" (Liebes and Grisek 1993: 197, my translation). Here we see that the speaker views television news as objective, his window on the world, an illusion reinforced by the material appearance of the television set, its shape and glass screen. He fails to see elements such as selection, camera position, editing decisions, etc.; he fails to see point of view, the television news not as objective reality but as a construct created by journalists, reflecting their perspective and the perspectives and directives of their editors, sponsors, and owners. This insight does not make the news untrue or untrustworthy. Rather, it describes an inherent feature of narrative: Everything is always and ineluctably told from a particular point of view, and interpretation necessitates comprehending and considering that point of view. (Context must always be considered in relation to text. In this case, the viewer was speaking at a time when Israel had a single, state-sponsored television channel. The keen national interest in breaking news and analysis meant that the channel had an exclusively powerful place in shaping the views of Israeli citizenry. This of course is no longer the case in today's viewing culture of multiple channels, including foreign news broadcasts.)

Often unnoticed but never unimportant, forms of address can be revealing fissures into hermeneutic activity. My *Newsweek* magazine has a tear-off postcard for potential subscribers. Respondents are told to check one of four squares: Mr./ Mrs. / Miss / Ms. Here we see how incorporation has effectively neutralized the feminist neologism "Ms." The title "Ms." was intended as the feminine equivalent of "Mr.," signaling gender but providing no additional personal information. This seemingly generous inclusion of the term, offering women three possible choices of self-description, actually restores the problem that "Ms." resolves. Male subscribers indicate only their maleness; women are either married, single, or feminist.

Analysis of syntax can reward the attentive reader. Feminist scholar and linguist Deborah Cameron offers us a hermeneutically rich example from the British newspaper *Daily Telegraph*: "A man who suffered head injuries when attacked by two men who broke into his home in Beckenham, Kent, early yesterday, was pinned down on the bed by intruders who took it in turns to rape his wife" (1990). This sentence about a rape has the victim's husband as its subject. Moreover, if we look at the modifiers we see that all description is devoted to the man. Similarly, the possessive is used twice: the intruders broke into *his home* and raped *his wife*. The wife is thus doubly objectified, identified only by a noun that labels her in terms of her marital status (*wife*, in contrast to her husband, labeled *man*). She is positioned as *his* in a parallel construction with the previous "*his home.*" The wife is thus a possession on the level of a home; her rape, like the break-in of his home, is a crime against the man, a violation of his property.

Having noted these features of this sentence, we then try to interpret them, restoring context to text. The sentence appeared as the lead in a story in a daily newspaper. One possible interpretation is that this sentence is a reflection of a male supremacist society, where wives, like homes, are the possessions of male subjectivity, where the objectification of women finds grammatical expression in this sentence from a daily newspaper. Another interpretation, not necessarily conflicting, emerges from a consideration of the sentence in its material context, a daily newspaper. Perhaps rape is so common in British culture that a report like this one would only attract readers if presented from a different angle, the presence of another victim, the helpless husband. The point of analysis of this sort, following entry through critical reading of textual fissures, is not to find a single definitive interpretation. Rather, it is to allow all possibly persuasive interpretations to emerge, validating or refuting them by anchoring them in close reading of the text.

The 1999 Israeli election propaganda offers an interesting exercise for interpretation. Early in the campaign, billboards on the streets of Jerusalem were covered with banners proclaiming [my translation]:

Barak will hand over
The Likud will hold on

The parallel construction here invites interpretation. (It is more effective in the original Hebrew, where each line is a two-word sentence: subject-verb. The rhythm of the Hebrew sentences is also compelling: "*Barak yimsor; Halikud yishmor.*") Ehud Barak, Labor party leader, is the subject of the first sentence; the parallel subject in the second sentence is the Likud party, not its leader. This imbalance, party leader named in the case of Labor, unnamed in the case of the Likud, is interesting. My interpretation of this imbalance is that the Likud sloganeers decided to lower the visibility of the party leader, Benjamin Netanyahu, who had become something of an electoral liability, even in the eyes of party loyalists. In its choice of syntactic subject, this slogan reflects—and enacts— that strategy. Moreover, the "handing over" (a negative action in popular Israeli parlance) is associated with a single man, Ehud Barak. By attributing the unpopular "handing over" to Barak and by not engaging in a polemic with the Labor party, the appeal of "holding on" under the leadership of the Likud party does not challenge party loyalties. A Labor party loyalist could dissociate himself from Barak during that crucial election without having to reevaluate his party affiliation. In a very close election with a seemingly equally split populace, choice of proper noun could thus help facilitate crossover voting.[12]

Shifting to the American political scene, the *International Herald Tribune* of 11 March 1999 provides us with headlines of interpretative interest. Reading through the fissures of a single day's headlines, we follow a basic move of rhetorical criticism, taking "account of the structures of the smallest discussable units of meaning and the ways in which these vary as they are put with other units" (Richards 1965: 8–9). The move here is two steps, first reading the individual headline in terms of stylistic features that invite interpretation, then analyzing the individual headline in the context of comparable units (the other headlines in that issue of that newspaper). Two headlines that day refer to prominent women with extensive public recognition in the United States, both of whom were running for public office at the time. One, describing Hillary Clinton's race for a New York Senate seat, proclaims: *See Hillary Run*. The other, describing Elizabeth Dole's bid for the Republican presidential nomination, declares: *Mrs. Dole Takes Step For White House Run.* All other headlines that day refer to male public figures, mentioning them by family name or title (*"Clinton Vows . . ."* [a reference to then-President Bill Clinton], (*"Prince Charles Stirs . . . ,"* *"Cohen and Jordan King Discuss . . . ,"* *"Iran's Leader Hails . . ."*). In the context of the *International Herald Tribune,* of American journalism in general, and of Hillary Clinton's campaign at that point, the first-person reference of *"See Hillary Run"* is somewhat irregular. (She later adopted the first-person appellation, using its familiarity to ameliorate her coldly distant public image.) Moreover, the register of the headline is that of a child's primer, the first reading textbook studied in school: on reading this headline, *See Spot Run* would be an immediate association for any adult American taught to read in the United States. ("Register" is the term linguists use to describe the correlation between an utterance and the context in which it is made, suiting language to circumstance in a socially appropriate manner, part of all socialization and recognizable to a native speaker.) This headline is doubly fissured for interpretation: Both appellation and register open the text to the attentive reader. My interpretation is that Hillary Clinton's candidacy is presented with a certain amount of disrespect. My textual anchors for this interpretation are in the combination of the first-name reference and the primary school register of the headline. Similarly, I note the problematic of the second headline referring to a woman candidate for public office that same day in that same newspaper. In 1999, Elizabeth Dole presented a newspaper editor with a problem like that of Hillary Clinton; both women, prominent in their own right, had husbands who were public figures at the time. Neither woman, therefore, could be referred to solely by her family name; the reader's assumption would be that the reference was to her husband. But "Mrs. Dole" is a choice; the reference could as well have been to "Elizabeth Dole" as, in our earlier example, Hillary Clinton could have been referred to by both first and family names. I interpret this second headline rhetorically as demeaning to Elizabeth Dole's presidential aspirations, identifying her only in terms of her marital status, perhaps even implying that Elizabeth Dole's candidacy owes more to her husband than to her own professional stature. I anchor my interpretation both in the choice of "Mrs. Dole" over "Elizabeth Dole" and in a comparison with the labels used in that day's headlines for male public figures (noted above). Again, I am not claiming that this disrespect or derision was intended by the writers of the headlines, solely that this is their effect. However, I am claiming that this effect is worth studying, and that close reading of this sort, opening texts through fissures like those I have been describing, reveals ideological sub-texts not necessarily visible on cursory reading.

Different texts invite different critical strategies. Narrative analy-sis (Genette 1980[1972]; Rimmon-Kenan 1989[1983]) focuses on larger textual units in addition to analyzing fissures such as those I describe above. The organization of narrative time offers two addi-tional thresholds of analytic entry: 1) the order of events as nar-rated (what inaugurates the narrative, what comes next to and/or after what); 2) the duration of narrated events (how much text compared to how much chronological time). Order can be revela-tory in indicating priorities and internal connections. A speaker's choices in ordering events are analyzed in comparison to a recon-structed chronology (Rosenthal 1993: 66–70), highlighting narra-tive selections (and silences). Beginnings are places of emphasis; juxtapositions offer glimpses of association.

Duration can also offer profitable textual entry. Comparison of how much text (lines or pages of written text, minutes of audio- or videotaped recordings) to the chronological time of the narrated event can be instructive. For example, Gabriele Rosenthal inter-prets the brevity (thirteen lines) of an account by an elderly Ger-man of a year of his adolescence spent in the Hitler Youth movement as significant in terms of the image of himself that he would like to impress upon his interviewer (Rosenthal 1993: 74–75). She interprets the constraint of his response to her request for his life story, told in less than a third of the time taken by most of her other subjects, to similar motives of image projection (72). The speaker's hesitancies and priorities reflected in duration thus give us access to subtexts that a speaker is perhaps unaware of or does not intend to communicate. In connection with other salient fis-sures, these may tell a story quite different from the one the speaker believes s/he is telling. The question "what does this fea-ture serve" is always brought to bear on textual elements, without aspersion—or speculation—regarding authorial intentionality.

These textual fissures are the tools used and extended to the longer unit of narrative in the following chapters.[13] The texts in this book (with a single exception in chapter 6) are narrated in the first person. My choice in narrowing the field to a single narrative mode enables me to sharpen analytic focus on uses of narrative point of view. In his articulation of the phenomenology of reading, George Poulet observes that "whenever I read, I mentally pronounce an I, and yet the I which I pronounce is not myself" (1969: 56). First-person narration brings together at least three "I"'s and not "I's" of this type (author, narrator, reader), a field rich in possibilities for hermeneutic entry.

Reading narrative voice ("the way in which the narrating itself is implicated in the narrative" [Genette 1980: 31]) and other fissures brings into view the ways in which a text creates its reader. In this sense, the eclectic method applied throughout this book is a pragmatic analysis, looking at "the text in a communicative context" (Adams 1985: 41). The author referred to is always perceived not as an individual historical personage but as a Foucaultian "system of constraint" by which "one impedes the free circulation, the free manipulation, the free composition, decomposition, and recomposition" of texts (Foucault 1980: 210, 209). Textual fissures are the marks of that textual constraint; this study traces their significance in both reading and writing narratives.⑭

This study is functionally divided in two.[15] Part I, Reading Exemplary Fissures: Strategies of Complicity and Resistance, considers ways in which texts elicit complicity and resistance in their readers through looking at four stylistic features. Chapters 1 and 2 look at two types of framing: authorial prefacing and narrative frames. Chapter 3 looks at textual voices, techniques of multiplicity and their effects. Chapter 4 considers an aspect of narrative time—temporary and permanent gaps—in relation to reader response. Thus Part I aims to exemplify techniques of textual entry and analytic anchoring, looking at fictional narratives as exemplary, not limiting. Until recently, literary studies have been the exclusive domain of this type of exegesis; today, its tools are increasingly borrowed by other disciplines. Walter Fisher views narration "as paradigmatic of human discourse" (1987: 98) and foundational for cross-disciplinary rhetorical theory. In his meditation on what he calls *The Literary Mind*, Mark Turner represents narrative as essentially human, originary, definitive and universal:

We imagine realities and construct meanings. The everyday mind performs these feats by means of mental processes that are literary and that have always been judged to be literary. Cultural meanings peculiar to a society often fail to migrate intact across anthropological or historical boundaries, but the basic mental processes that make these meanings possible are universal. (1996: 11)

The fictional narratives that provide the texts of Part I extend the application of stylistic features discussed and exemplified in this introductory chapter, providing longer and more sustained exercises in critical reading through narrative fissures. It is my hope that my greater goal does not stand or fall on whether the reader agrees with all my analyses of individual texts; they are intended as illustrative, not definitive.

With the exception of chapter 5, the narratives studied here are fictional. The "family resemblance" (Ricoeur 1981: 287–95) of fictional narrative and non-narrative is the basis for their conflation in this study. Part II, with its focus on writing the metanarrative, reinstates the separation between these two types of narrative (ethnography, the subject of chapter 5, and fictional ethnography, that of chapter 6) only to conflate them again in the epilogue on ethical aspects of narrative strategies. To borrow Paul Ricoeur's words, in moving through its first two parts to its epilogue, this study follows as "the world of fiction leads us to the heart of the real world of action" and back again (1981: 295). The narrative strategies of fictional texts are shared by nonfictional narrative, and their study is meant to suggest methods and uses to readers in diverse fields.

Part II hopes to do the same for writers. Labeling writing about narrative "metanarrative," this section outlines directions for reflexive writing. As Clifford Geertz states: "The difficulty is that the oddity of constructing texts ostensibly scientific out of experiences so broadly biographical, which is after all what ethnographers do, is thoroughly obscured" (1988: 10). Attempting to penetrate this obscurity, Part II highlights rhetorical decisions and their consequences in ethnography and ethnographic fiction, in both fictional and nonfictional texts. This section is by design more tentative than the first, mapping rhetorical moves in order to suggest the outlines of a genre of reflectively reflexive metanarrative.

Most tentative of all in the progression of this book (my metanarrative) is the final chapter, not given the status of "chapter" but framed for my reader as "epilogue." Following Paul Ricoeur's insight that "there is no ethically neutral narrative" (1992: 115) and my own reading of the ethical implications of two ethnographic fictions of ritual sacrifice in chapter 6, the epilogue defines and interprets a single key fissure—narrative resolution—and its implications in three similarly situated contemporary fictions. Using the reading strategies discussed and applied throughout this book, the epilogue aims to provoke thought and invite discussion of the important and undertheorized ethical aspects of narrative.[16]

The progressively tentative nature of this book reflects, I believe, the "state of the art" at the interdisciplinary nexus of narrative. The reading skills of literary studies are readily available and easily learned (Part I); incorporating them in self-reflexive writing is beginning to form a distinctive genre (Part II). The ethical aspects of this reading and this writing that are raised in the epilogue will always defy resolution, and will equally necessitate attentive consideration. In structure too this book attempts to be rhetorically self-reflexive, enacting, together with its reader, applications and implications of contemporary thought on narrative.

Part I
Reading Exemplary Fissures: Strategies of Complicity and Resistance

Reading Exemplary Fissures: Strategies of Complicity and Resistance

> . . . the writing of the text anticipates the readings to come.
> —Ricoeur (1984: 166)

PART I EXTENDS THE APPLICATION OF NARRATIVE FISSURES FROM THE small textual units of the introduction to the largest unit of narrative. The aim remains the same: bringing into view features that can function as fissures of hermeneutic entry and demonstrating the reading path thus opened. This section is divided into four chapters, demonstrating critical reading of narrative mode by focusing on strategies of narration as narrative fissures. In a sense, Part I is structured mimetically, building a narrative of its own. Chapters 1 and 2 focus on narrative beginnings, chapter 3 on middles, and chapter 4 on the narrative aftermath of temporary and permanent gaps. To put that less figuratively: chapter 1 reads authorial prefacing as a fissure, using Mary Shelley's *Frankenstein* (1817) and its two prefatory texts; chapter 2 looks at narrative framing through a reading of Henry James's *Turn of the Screw* (1898); chapter 3 uses Bakhtin's concept of "heteroglossia" as the key fissure of two contemporaneous novels of South Africa in transition, Nadine Gordimer's *My Son's Story* and J. M. Coetzee's *Age of Iron*, both published in 1990; and chapter 4 uses temporary and permanent gaps as its central fissure, reading three novels of very different periods and societies that share a central gap, Michael Dorris's *A Yellow Raft in Blue Water* (1987), Reynolds Price's *Kate Vaiden* (1986), and Daniel Defoe's *Moll Flanders* (1722).

All four chapters interpret a key textual fissure in relation to narrative mode and the ways in which those authorial choices elicit responses of complicity and resistance. My concepts of complicit and resisting readers have evolved from Richard Ohmann's observation that "[l]iterary mimesis implicates the reader in an imagined

society by making him party to the acts that imply it" (1973: 102).
Extending Ohmann's analysis, I posit two readers, one resisting
and one complicit, as a text's ideal or implied readers, and track
those constructs through four varieties of narrative fissure. The
reader I am calling a "resisting reader"[1] is one who is cued by a text
to resist the text's narrator. The reader I am calling a "complicit
reader" is one who is cued to follow a text's narrator without questioning his/her reliability.

I suggest these terms (complicit/resisting) as an alternative to
Wayne Booth's reliable and unreliable narrators (the reliable narrator being one who "speaks for or acts in accordance with the norms
of the work [which is to say, the implied author's norms]," the unreliable narrator one who "does not" [1983: 158–59]). The problem
with the concept of reliability is in its application. Reliability is often
attributed to omniscient narrators and unreliability to character
narrators, leading to a conflation of omniscience with reliability and
first-person narration with unreliability (Yacobi 1981: 120–21). It
is this mistaken conflation that undermines the usefulness of the
concept of reliability, and which I seek to repair by focusing on
reader response as it is encoded in the text. Complicit or resisting
readers are not cognate with reliable or unreliable narrators; they
are also not the function of a single narrative mode.

An author's choice of narrative mode is an act of selection that
exposes "the intentionality of the text, . . . what the text does,
rather than what the text is meant to mean" (Iser 1993: 6). Complicity or resistance in readers is forged by the relationship between
world and text and between a text's implied author and its narrator.
Axiomatic to this study is an author-reader collaboration. Eliciting
complicity or resistance to a narrator is a rhetorical strategy always
aimed at enhancing that real-world collaboration toward realizing
the potential of any text.[2]

Many of the disciplines now concerning themselves with narratives (the social sciences, medicine, law) interpret the narratives
of first-person informants. First-person texts often constitute the
primary portion of the raw material transformed by ethnographers
and others into their metanarratives. Part I aims to demonstrate
ways in which my concept of narrative fissure as textual entry can
be applied in interpreting these primary-source narratives. The
narratives of Part I are varieties of mimetic fiction, used here as
"models of interaction," a means of acquiring "the narrative un-

derstanding nourished by literature" (Ricoeur 1992: 162). The substantive mimesis of these texts is what allows me to suggest application of these reading tools to real-life narratives.[3]

In order to limit the textual field by creating a common ground, I have restricted the texts discussed in this section to a single narrative strategy, that of cross-gendering, using the accessible fissures provided by cross-gendering as an exemplary case for critical reading of first-person narratives. Cross-gendered narratives are texts that are authored by individuals of one sex and told in the first-person as if by a person of the other sex.[4] The ventriloquism of this narrative strategy provides a fissure through which critical readers can view how male and female authors exploit the conventions of gender-marking in these narratives, extending concepts of grammatical gender-marking to narrative fiction.

Thus each of the four chapters in this section enters the narratives it analyzes through two fissures, one unique to the particular chapter and one (cross-gendering) shared by all. By limiting the reading field to cross-gendered narratives, one variant of first-person narration, I hope to sharpen issues of reader-narrator complicity and resistance. While all texts viewed here share a powerful central stylistic device (cross-gendered narration), they create markedly different reader-narrator relationships. The similarities and differences in reader-response—and their textual triggers—are the purview of Part I.

First then, a few words about the shared fissure of cross-gendering: The concepts of grammatical gender-marking that I am borrowing and extending in these chapters are those that have traditionally preserved (and hidden) male linguistic dominance, concepts such as "generic man" and the "unmarked" masculine pronoun as features of "correct usage." The myth of the generic man (the base of such compound words as "mankind" and "manpower") reads these terms as gender-neutral. That of the unmarked masculine pronoun claims the same neutrality for the application of the third-person masculine pronoun to both sexes unless a specific gender-marking is intended. Thus, as Simone de Beauvoir wrote in 1949,

> man represents both the positive and the neutral, as is indicated by the common use of man to designate human beings in general; whereas woman represents only the negative, defined by limiting criteria, without reciprocity . . . there is an absolute human type, the masculine. (xv)

This cultural gender-marking is the grid against which male and female authors use cross-gendering in narration to different effect.

In broad terms, women authors of cross-gendered fiction exploit what Jeannette Silveira (1980: 165–78) calls the "people = male bias" of gender-marked language, speaking in the first-person as men to gain the normative position of this cultural and linguistic bias. The unmarked masculine "has two meanings, . . . the explicit absence of 'feminine' in the meaning 'male human being' [and] also . . . 'human being' in general" (Greenberg 1966: 25). It is to attain the status of "human being in general" that women use cross-gendering in narration. Cross-gendering in mimetic fiction offers women writers in Western patriarchal societies (social systems that enable men to dominate women) a way of speaking in the dominant mode while remaining in the margin. Perhaps it is the multivoiced potential of narrative fiction that accounts for the significant contribution of women to this art form.

Male-authored cross-gendered texts exploit a different feature of gender-marking, what Joseph Greenberg calls "defectivation," where "[t]he marked category may simply lack certain categories present in the unmarked category" (29). In the case of gender-marking, what the feminine lacks is the universality of "human being." The male author gains a perch on the margins of humanity by speaking through a female voice; the "defect" or "lack" of both masculine and general human status is used here to achieve a vantage point on the periphery of male-dominated power structures. The prevailing patriarchal structures of our society preserve the potential marginality of women as "the silent but enabling condition of writing" that Elizabeth Harvey observes in the Renaissance (1992: 78).

In this connection, it is interesting to listen to the remarks of two contemporary artists on their storytelling strategies. For both men, writing of two very different societies, women retain the position of marginality that facilitates storytelling. In an interview with *The New York Times* (19 November 1995), British playwright David Hare explains that women serve as the "moral center" of his politically and socially conscious plays about late-twentieth-century England because "they stand outside a man's world and so can see it more clearly." Israeli photographer-director David Benchetrit discusses a similar choice in an interview with the *Jerusalem Post* (3 July 1992). He explains why his film on contemporary Palestinian society, *Through the Veil of Exile*, focuses on women in that society. "The only way to penetrate the soul of this society is via its women. The men in such a conservative society sell ideas, not themselves. I wanted to pass on doubts, and male members of a society in struggle wouldn't give me that."

Simply put, cross-gendering in classical fiction is used by male authors to position themselves on the margin of the society they are describing, whereas it is used by female authors to gain a normative position relative to society. Thus for women authors the exploitation of cultural gender-marking in cross-gendered narrative fiction is similar to what sociologist Erving Goffman calls passing—where a person "conceals information about his real social identity, receiving and accepting treatment based on false suppositions concerning himself." For male authors it is a situation of reverse passing— "concealment of creditable facts" (1970:58). For both male and female authors, this manipulation of cultural concepts of gender in narrative mode is used to shape the reader's attitude toward the text.

Roland Barthes describes reading as "rewriting the text of the work within the text of our lives" (1985: 101). Cross-gendered narratives, with their open secret of ventriloquism across gender roles, bring cultural gender constructs to the reader's consciousness for reassessment. Since we "speak, read, and write from a gender-marked place within our social and cultural context" (Furman 1980: 52), the question "who is speaking?" in a text must be considered together with the question "who is being addressed?" What has the author gained by his or her choice of narrative structure?[5]

Exploitation of gender-marking by authors of both sexes is effected in similar modality (the choice of cross-gendered narration)

> because similar forms can be used by non-dominant groups as strategies of resistance, which are not more (and no less) compromised by this similarity than is the case with ideological complexes in the discourse of the dominant. . . . If the same text or topic can have such ambiguous or different ideological meanings depending on the play of forces in their semiotic context, then we clearly cannot assume a single automatic value of "dominant" or "resistant" for any ideological form. (Hodge 1990: 17)

Thus it is not the sex of the author of a cross-gendered text that determines its ideological position in an automatic and essentialist homology. Rather, analysis of the open secret of gender crossing in these texts reveals both the ideological position of the individual text and the gendered differences of writing. My choice of cross-gendering as a shared exemplary fissure in studying narrative mode against other key narrative fissures is prompted by the higher visibility of the open secret of narrative ventriloquism in such fiction. But the claim I am making for the role of narrative mode in reader response applies to all other narrative strategies as well.[6] It is not the gesture of cross-gendering itself that challenges concepts of cultural gender-determination; cross-gendering can be equally conservative or subversive. Interpretation of this strategy as it is used in specific texts can give us insight into the ideological positioning revealed by this choice, while reminding us that there is no formulaic connection between any particular fissure and an interpretation. In the essential analytic relationship between text and context, the choice of cross-gendering as narrative mode can be understood only in its specific context. The forged field of the cross-gendered narratives of Part I allows me to contextualize these readings in terms of a second narrative fissure, chapter-specific, reading the choice of cross-gendered narration in relation to prefacing, framing, textual voices, and gaps. All four chapters look at gender-marking in relation to a particular stylistic device, viewed here as a fissure through which to begin critical reading and analysis of how complicity and/or resistance are elicited. As Shoshana Felman instructs us, "the key . . . is <u>learning how to read . . . structures of address</u>" (1993: 157, original emphasis). This "learning how to read" is the essence and the substance of the following chapters.

1

On Prefacing

MARY SHELLEY'S *FRANKENSTEIN* (1817) IS AN EXEMPLARY TEXT FOR THE
central concern of this chapter demonstrating the coupled fissures
of cross-gendering and prefaces. Her oblique novel uses three
cross-gendered narratives preceded by two prefatory frames to tell
its story, and this chapter examines the purport of each of these
choices. Following the author's lead, we will enter her novel
through her 1817 preface and 1831 introduction, reading them together as a fissure through which the novel's text and context are
seen in sharper focus.

In the preface to the 1817 edition of Mary Shelley's *Frankenstein*, the author addresses an implied reader's concern for authenticity and morality. In a first-person authorial voice, the preface
enacts a preemptive positioning of the novel's reader:

> I have thus endeavoured to preserve the truth of the elementary princi-
> ples of human nature, while I have not scrupled to innovate upon their
> combinations. . . . I am by no means indifferent to the manner in which
> whatever moral tendencies exist in the sentiments or characters it con-
> tains shall affect the reader; yet my chief concern in this respect has
> been limited to the avoiding the enervating effects of the novels of the
> present day and to the exhibition of the amiableness of domestic af-
> fection, and the excellence of universal virtue. (5)

As we learn in Mary Shelley's introduction to the 1831 edition of
her novel, the voice prefacing its first edition with an interpretation
of it as "the exhibition of the amiableness of domestic affection,
and the excellence of universal virtue" is that of her husband, the
poet Percy Bysshe Shelley. Writing about the authorship of *Frankenstein* fourteen years after its first publication, she states:

> I certainly did not owe the suggestion of one incident, nor scarcely of
> one train of feeling, to my husband, and yet but for his incitement, it

would never have taken the form in which it was presented to the
world. From this declaration I must except the preface. As far as I can
recollect, it was entirely written by him. (11)

Percy Shelley's appropriation of Mary's "I" in the preface to her
first novel offers an important insight into the narrative structure
of the novel.[1] *Frankenstein* is an epistolary novel narrated by R.
Walton, who is exploring Arctic waters and writing to his sister in
England. Walton's narration encircles that of Victor Frankenstein,
who tells Walton his story as he is dying. Embedded in Frankenstein's story and encircled by both Walton and Frankenstein's narratives is the story of a year in the life of the monster that
Frankenstein created, told to Frankenstein by the monster in an
effort to persuade Frankenstein to create a mate for him. All three
narratives, Walton's, Frankenstein's, and the monster's, are told in
the first person; all are male. Why does Mary Shelley tell her story
this way? What is the story that she is telling?

In her 1831 introduction to the novel (written long after her husband's accidental death), Mary Shelley tells us the history of its creation. Initially undertaking the task of writing a ghost story to
entertain one another, Byron and Percy Shelley quickly dropped
out of the collective holiday recreation. In a comment revealing her
attitude toward writing fiction as inferior to the writing of poetry,
and herself as inferior to her companions, Mary Shelley explains
that the "illustrious poets . . . , annoyed by the platitude of prose,
speedily relinquished their uncongenial task" (9). Pressure to produce remained, however, on Mary. ("*Have you thought of a story?*
I was asked each morning, and each morning I was forced to reply
with a mortifying negative" [9, original italics].) That pressure had
always been part of her marriage. As she explains:

> My husband, however, was from the first, very anxious that I should
> prove myself worthy of my parentage, and enrol myself on the page of
> fame. He was for ever inciting me to obtain literary reputation, which
> even on my own part I cared for then. . . . At this time he desired that I
> should write, not so much with the idea that I could produce any thing
> worthy of notice, but that he might himself judge how far I possessed
> the promise of better things hereafter. Still I did nothing. (8)

The daughter of two authors, expected to write both by others and
by herself, found herself unable to write, as her husband wished
her to so he might judge her talents.

In the description of her childhood writing given in her 1831 introduction to the novel, writing about herself as a child "of two persons of distinguished literary celebrity,"[2] she tells us that she "scribbled" from an early age. She makes a distinction between writing and what she calls dreaming. "What I wrote [in childhood] was intended at least for one other eye—my childhood's companion and friend; but my dreams were all my own; I accounted for them to nobody; they were my refuge when annoyed—my dearest pleasure when free" (7, my emphasis).

Both in writing for her childhood companion and writing for the companion of her early adult life, Mary Shelley expresses the constriction and loss of autonomy she feels in the illocutionary act, as opposed to the freedom of dreams untold. She tells of "that blank incapability of invention which is the greatest misery of authorship, when dull Nothing replies to our anxious invocations" (9), and of the "mortification" she felt at having to admit daily to writer's block. She then describes a sleepless night during which the story that became *Frankenstein* came to her in what she calls a "waking dream" (11). Having "dreamt" her story, she tells of how she "began [writing] that day with the words, *It was on a dreary night of November*" (p. 11, original italics). These words do not, however, begin her novel; they begin the fifth chapter of Victor Frankenstein's twenty-four-chapter narrative, which is preceded by four chapters of explication and by Walton's frame narrative. The narrative structure of *Frankenstein*, three concentric and embedded narratives, reflects Shelley's pressing concern for authenticating one's narrative—a concern that all three narrators in turn express.

Walton, the Arctic explorer writing letters home, is the first narrator to express anxieties about communication and reception. Writing, he states in the letters to his sister that begin the framing narrative, "is a poor medium for the communication of feeling" (16). He "cannot describe" his feelings and finds them "impossible to communicate" (18) in his letters. However, distinguishing between writing of feeling and of fact, he seems confident in his ability "to record [in those same letters], as nearly as possible in his own words," the story of another, his transcript of Victor Frankenstein's deathbed caveat. Walton also expresses confidence in the reception of this transcript, asserting that it "will doubtless afford . . . [its reader] the greatest pleasure" (26).

At the novel's end, after the narrative of Victor Frankenstein and that of his monster, Mary Shelley returns to her frame narrative and has Walton resume the letters to his sister with which the novel begins, his final letter dated nine months after the first.[3] Having finished the "transcription" of Victor Frankenstein's tale and turning again to address his remarks to his sister, Walton asserts the authenticity of his notes of the scientist's account. He states that Frankenstein, though on his deathbed, had "corrected and augmented them in many places" (178). Further proofs of authenticity are provided by the scientist. Though Walton testifies that Victor Frankenstein's story "is connected and told with an appearance of the simplest truth," Frankenstein, in his turn, authenticates his narrative by extratextual documentation, showing Walton letters that the monster had given him. It is these letters, in addition to his own sighting of the monster, that give Walton (Frankenstein's audience) "a greater conviction of the truth of his narrative than his asseverations, however earnest and connected" (178). This story illustrates a lack of confidence in what Foucault has usefully termed the "author-function" in controlling the reception of narrative (1980: 209–10),[4] thus necessitating reliance on sources external and additional to the narrative. The dynamic tensions of narration and reception are again articulated and enacted in the monster's story, the center of these concentric narratives.

Frankenstein's monster seeks to augment the perlocutionary force of his narrative (Searle 1969). He needs to persuade, not just to be heard. ("How can I move thee? . . . Let your compassion be moved," he tells his creator.) But his first task is to get his audience to listen and understand, to increase the illocutionary force of his speech, as he reiterates in what we read as the opening paragraphs of his tale ("I entreat you to hear me," "Listen to my tale . . . hear me. . . . Listen to me, Frankenstein" [84–85]). Mid-narrative, the monster promises extratextual authentication of his narrative ["I have copies of these letters; . . . Before I depart, I will give them to you, they will prove the truth of my tale" (105)], as do Frankenstein and Walton. All three narrators express a lack of confidence in the author-function to determine the reception of their narratives, the same unease that their author implies in her stated preference for dreams, "accounted for . . . to nobody" (7). *Frankenstein*, Mary Shelley's dream turned prose, crosses the divide between dreaming and writing that the author had created in her childhood and attempts to communicate what she had previously considered "all my own" (7).

Complicating this initial crossing for Mary Shelley is her audience of what she calls "illustrious poets." We can get some sense of this in listening to the compliment to Byron ventriloquized by Percy Shelley through Mary in the preface to the first edition of her novel. Referring to the "illustrious poets" who were her companions and her audience, the author (Percy speaking as Mary) declares that "a tale from the pen of one [of her illustrious companions—Byron] would be far more acceptable to the public than anything I can ever hope to produce" (6). To facilitate her move from dreaming to writing, translating dream into prose, Mary Shelley creates her frame narrative. She dresses her dream as the narrative of an explorer who becomes the agent of its transmission.

The novel's first two narrators, Walton and Frankenstein, are in many ways character-doubles. They are portrayed in similar terms. Both men testify to "ardent curiosity" (13, 31, 34, 38), to preferring glory to wealth (15, 34), and to being self-taught (16, 34). Both satisfy their curiosity while endangering others, in what they both subsequently recognize as "mad schemes" (181, 140–41, 45). This similarity is insisted on by Frankenstein as the motive for telling his tale. He responds to Walton's short autobiography by exclaiming: "Unhappy man! Do you share my madness? Have you drank also of the intoxicating draught? Hear me—let me reveal my tale, and you will dash the cup from your lips!" (24).

"[P]eople tell their stories (which they do not know or cannot speak) through others' stories" (Felman 1993: 18). The doubling of R. Walton and Victor Frankenstein is extended and repeated in the novel, embracing both another character, the monster, and their author. Structurally, Frankenstein's tale is also that of another, his monster, just as Walton's is that of Frankenstein, and all three comprise the tale of Mary Shelley's "waking dream." This structure of concentric narratives encloses the key narrative at its center, that of the monster. It is the monster's narrative that I read as Mary Shelley's story, the story of *Frankenstein*.[5]

The monster tells his creator his story of language acquisition, describing himself as a silent listener to De Lacey family conversations as he hides in an adjacent shed and secretly observes their daily lives. Having been persecuted for his deformity and rendered mute by the lack of a common language, the monster learns by observation and imitation (95). Mary Shelley describes herself in a similar situation during the period when she was looking for a ghost story to write to entertain her companions Shelley and Byron while spending rainy days together in Switzerland. "Many and long were the conversations between Lord Byron and Shelley, to which I was a devout but nearly silent listener," she writes in her introduction (10). The monster expresses a similarly devout attitude toward the conversation he overhears, calling it "a godlike science" (95). Frustrated in his attempts "to express my sensations in my own mode," he withdrew as "the uncouth and inarticulate sounds which broke from me frightened me into silence again" (88). Not finding his "own mode," breaking out of that silence becomes possible for the monster only via the borrowed language he acquires through imitating his neighbors. Mary Shelley's monster is in the situation of a member of a muted group, whose "perceptions . . . are [to some extent] unstatable in the idiom of the dominant group. In order to be heard, muted group members must learn the dominant idiom and attempt to articulate within it, even though this attempt will inevitably lead to some loss of meaning" (Crawford and Chaffin: 21).[6] The monster diligently studies his neighbors' speech, recognizing that "although I eagerly longed to discover myself to the cottagers, I ought not to make the attempt until I had first become master of their language; which knowledge might enable me to make them overlook the deformity of my figure" (96–97).

In language that evokes that of both previous narrators (self-described autodidacts), the monster relates how he taught himself to read by diligent study of books he found in the woods (108). Describing his initiation into the reading process, the monster also describes the relationship of muted and dominant groups in cultural transmission: "As I read, however, I applied much personally to my own feelings and condition. I found myself similar, yet at the same time strangely unlike to the beings concerning whom I read, and to whose conversation I was a listener. I sympathised with, and partly understood them, but I was unformed in mind" (109). Some essences remain untranslatable, while members of muted groups assume the inferiority inevitable in their placement in this binary and hierarchical relationship. It is the monster who must master the language of his neighbors in the hope of ending his persecution and his consequent isolation on the margins of society, symbolized geographically by his habitation, a shed outside the De Lacey family cottage, itself on the outskirts of a village.

Mary Shelley tells this story of coming to language and groping for entry into the dominant group through the mediation of a wealthy English adventurer, R. Walton. She thus encases her "waking dream" in a normative voice who attests to the fact that the "tale is connected and told with an appearance of the simplest truth." The veracity of the monster's tale is supported by Walton's witnessing. He tells of seeing both the monster himself and letters of Felix De Lacey and his beloved Safie copied by the monster (178). This need for evidence reflects the author's unease in her own mastery of narrative in the dominant mode. Read through the prefatory frame of her introduction, it also reflects Mary Shelley's concerns about the potential reception of her work, written "not so much with the idea that I could produce any thing worthy of notice, but that he [Shelley] might himself judge how far I possessed the promise of better things hereafter" (8).

Frankenstein is dedicated to Mary Shelley's father, William Godwin, in a dedication that reads:

To
William Godwin
author of Political Justice, Caleb Williams, etc.
These volumes
Are respectfully inscribed
by
The Author

Mary Shelley does not mention Godwin in her introduction to the 1831 edition except to describe herself as "the daughter of two persons of distinguished literary celebrity" (p. 7). It is the shadow of her husband, not her father, that hangs over that introduction, just as it is the hand of Percy Shelley that wrote the preface to the original edition. But it is Percy Shelley whom Godwin shadows. In an unpublished review of *Frankenstein*, Percy Shelley praises the novel by comparing it to *Caleb Williams* (quoted in Veeder 1986: 226–27). He goes on to note (using the first-person plural for himself) that the novel "reminds us, indeed, somewhat of the style and character of that admirable writer, to whom the author has dedicated his work, and whose productions he seems to have studied."

Having ventriloquized the preface of the novel through its author, Percy here erases her gender, referring to the author in the masculine third-person. This erasure cannot possibly be considered unmarked. To my mind, it marks the site of Mary Shelley's struggle to translate her dreams ("all my own") into writing. Her "waking dream" is told through the mediation of Walton as her novel is prefaced and edited by her husband, speaking in her voice.[7]

For Percy Shelley, Victor Frankenstein is "the victim whose history . . . [the novel] relates" (quoted in Veeder: 225); he is the novel's "hero" (Shelley's preface to *Frankenstein*: 5). In his preface to the novel, Percy Shelley claims for the work "the exhibition of the amiableness of domestic affection" (5), an interpretation that he pursues in his review of the novel. There he claims it displays "sentiments . . . so affectionate and innocent . . . pictures of domestic manners . . . of the most simple and attaching character . . . pathos . . . irresistible and deep" (unpublished review, quoted in Veeder: 226). The novel, he claims, has a "direct moral," and it is: "Treat a person ill, and he will become wicked" (quoted in Veeder: 226). The monster, for Percy Shelley, is "an abortion and an anomaly"; "the circumstances of his existence . . . monstrous and uncommon" (266).

The "circumstances of his existence" are monstrous but not uncommon; they reflect those of his author. As I read the novel, the monster's story is not an anomaly, but rather the story of the nineteenth-century woman writer, a member of that muted group struggling, as the monster does, "to express my sensations in my own mode" (88), while conceding, as the monster does, the need for mastery of the dominant language (96). Writing in 1831 as an older woman and a more experienced writer than the author of *Frankenstein*, many years beyond the young girl who shared her writing but not her dreams, Mary Shelley declares it "true that I am very averse to bringing myself forward in print" (7). She justifies her introduction by noting that it had been solicited by her publishers. Maintaining her childhood split between writing and dreaming, she declares that her introduction "will be confined to such topics as have connections with my authorship alone," not "a personal intrusion" (7).

In the nineteenth century, writing in the dominant mode meant writing in a universal (a word Percy Shelley uses in both his preface to and review of *Frankenstein*), not personal, mode. Mary Shelley's uneasy accommodation is reflected both in her writing of the novel and in its introduction. Though Percy Shelley, disguised as Mary, describes her aims in writing the novel in terms of morality, Mary Shelley's introduction speaks of it as the writing of a dream—while declaring that she seeks to avoid "a personal intrusion" in her highly personal narrative. Similarly, this crossing of a childhood divide between dreaming and writing is negotiated through male narrators doubling interestingly with their author. Percy Shelley asserts moral value for his wife's novel; Mary Shelley herself makes no such assertions. This concentrically narrated, triply cross-gendered novel uses blanks in the narrative that force the reader out of "our habitual frame of reference" by disrupting "good continuation" (Iser 1978: 186), thereby forcing the reader to more active participation. Reading *Frankenstein* through the fissure of the preface and introduction exposes tensions echoed structurally in the novel and articulated in the direct speech of its narrative voices.

A similar tension between Mary Shelley's novel and the one Percy Shelley would like us to read is also revealed in the textual articulations of the novel's science. As noted above, the scientist of Mary Shelley's dream is referred to as "the artist" in her introduction (10). In her novel, the experiments of Victor Frankenstein are given no support outside of the narrative. Rather, he is frequently referred to as an artist of "unhallowed arts" (for example, 76). An assertion of scientism and the only appeal to extratextual and scientific sources in *Frankenstein* is that written by Percy Shelley in the novel's 1817 preface. Speaking as Mary in the first sentence of the preface to the original edition of the novel, he (speaking as she) asserts that "[t]he event on which this fiction is founded has been supposed, by Dr. Darwin, and some of the physiological writers of Germany, as not of impossible occurrence" (5). Despite this instance of external authorization claimed for the novel by Percy Shelley, the narrators of *Frankenstein* gain their authenticity by repetition and intratextual similarity, not extratextual validation. This is precisely what Percy Shelley does not see in his view of the monster as "an abortion and an anomaly." The fissures of narrative mode and prefatory framing bring this clearly into view. The novel insists on the shared qualities of its three narrators, and the preface and introduction allow us to view ways in which their creator is reflected in her narrators. All three of her narrators are curious, diligent, and self-educated; all recognize the problem of legitimating their narratives. All refer to another genre—the letters of Felix and Safie, copied by the monster and passed from narrator to narrator—as proof of the veracity (and therefore value) of his narrative. The monster is not anomalous; through him, and through his companion narrators in this concentric novel, we glimpse the nineteenth-century woman writer. Adding the perspective of viewing this choice of narrative mode through the fissure of hermeneutic entry provided by Percy Shelley's 1817 preface and Mary Shelley's 1831 introduction, this parallel can be clearly seen.

The gender-crossing of *Frankenstein* aims for reader complicity by augmenting the illocutionary force of the novel, positioning the frame narrator in the normative position of a male member of a patriarchal society, a person of some wealth and authority, who attests to the truth of the tale (178). Similarly, in the original edition of the novel, this narrative crossing is preceded by a ventriloquized preface. The author of *Frankenstein* has the value of her work authorized for her as she cedes the author-function of *Frankenstein* to her husband in the preface to the original edition. Long after his accidental death, she reasserts this value in her own introduction to her novel's second edition. Mary Shelley, struggling to find voice in the generic tradition of her father's novel *Things As They Are, or the Adventures of Caleb Williams*, writing too in the shadow of her poet-husband, reminds us that "things as they are" are often not what they seem.

2

On Framing

THIS CHAPTER SHIFTS THE FOCUS OF CHAPTER ONE FROM THE COUPLED fissures of prefatory framing and cross-gendering to narrative framing, where prefatory positioning has moved within the narrative.[1] Prefatory and introductory frames are author-identified and presented in distinctly separated texts. Narrative framing functions similarly to prefaces (in dialogic exchange with the central narrative), while constituting part of that central narrative. Henry James's *The Turn of the Screw* (1898) provides us with an interesting text for reading through the fissures of cross-gendered narration and narrative framing. James uses two male narrators (in first-person narration and in direct speech) in the frame narrative preceding the first-person female narrator of the central narrative. His narrative frame is left open (in contrast to *Frankenstein*, for example, where Walton begins and ends the novel). Reading through these fissures, we see ways in which selection and manipulation of narrative voices create a text's implied reader.[2] Exposing the ways the narrative creates reader compliance with and resistance to its textual voices brings into view the ideological base of this Gothic novella, which James called his "perfectly independent and irresponsible fiction" (1986 [1898]: 35).

The Turn of the Screw uses a layered narrative of two brief preliminary frames preceding the main narrative, an ambiguous tale of child abuse. The frame narrative is told by an unnamed narrative "I" who brings us the story of the telling of the governess's tale by the narrator Douglas. Both narrators precede the governess and color our response to her tale. James's gender-crossing occurs in the central narrative, the third narrator of this story, a former governess. Neither male narrator resumes his opening narrative after the governess's tale, creating a layered narrative, an open-bottom frame and the source of the story's ambiguity. The ghosts of the

governess's narrative are not finally supported or denied by an authorial voice or that of other narrators or characters, leaving the
narrator alone in voicing her ghostly vision and leaving the reader
similarly unsupported.

Why did James choose to tell this tale this way? In his *Notebooks*
James outlined the story he was told and that he transformed in his
Turn:

> Note here the ghost-story told me at Addington . . . by the Archbishop
> of Canterbury: the mere vague, undetailed, faint sketch of it—being all
> he had been told (very badly and imperfectly), by a lady who had no art
> of relation, and no clearness: the story of the young children (indefinite
> number and age) left to the care of servants in an old country-house,
> through the death, presumably, of parents. The servants, wicked and
> depraved, corrupt and deprave the children; the children are bad, full
> of evil, to a sinister degree. The servants <u>die</u> (the story vague about the
> way of it) and their apparitions, figures, return to haunt the house <u>and</u>
> children, to whom they seem to beckon, whom they invite and solicit,
> from across dangerous places, the deep ditch of a sunk fence, etc. —so
> that the children may destroy themselves, lose themselves, by respond-
> ing, by getting into their power. So long as the children are kept from
> them, they are not lost; but they try and try and try, these evil pres-
> ences, to get hold of them. It is a question of the children "coming over
> to where they are." It is all obscure and imperfect, the picture, the
> story, but there is a suggestion of strangely gruesome effect in it. The
> story to be told—tolerably obviously—by an outside spectator, observer.
> (Matthiessen and Murdock 1961: 178–79, original emphasis)

The story as noted by James does not mention a governess. The
agent of the sentence "[s]o long as the children are kept from [the
ghosts]" (which becomes the governess in James's story) is not
stated, and James's final note suggests a third-person narrator. The
selection of the governess as narrator indicates that James's story
changed from that described in the *Notebooks*. These changes deriving from the character of the governess provide the fissure
through which I interpret *Turn of the Screw* as a portrait of hysteria, an attempt to enter into the subjectivity of the hysteric.[3] Late-
nineteenth-century ambivalence toward the hysteric is reflected in
the narrative structure of the novella, allowing James to speak in
her imagined voice yet leaving that voice without authorial support,
the governess (or the hysteric) presented as an object of homosocial
exchange in a manuscript given by one male narrator to another.

In the first frame narrative of the story, Douglas responds to a ghost story (where a ghost appeared to a young child) he has just heard. The story, in his view, effected "another turn of the screw" (145) of the strange tales being exchanged by the gathered company, the fictional audience. Someone in his audience affirms that his proposed story of two children thus afflicted "give[s] two turns." What is the effect of adding a woman to this narrative stew?

In the narrative that precedes the governess's main narrative (her narrative is represented as a manuscript original), the fictional addressees are both women and men. The women in this fictional audience are gratuitously ridiculed and silenced, an attitude that the narrative presents as self-explanatory and does not justify. Douglas describes the unique "dreadfulness" of the governess's tale and in response, "cried one of the women [in his audience]," "Oh how delicious!" The narrator tells us that Douglas "took no notice of her" and that "[i]t was to me in particular that he appeared to propound this" (146). Circulation of the governess's narrative serves homosocial ends, reinforcing the bonding between the two male narrators of the frame. This privileging of the first narrator by the second continues, as he tells us that Douglas "continued to fix me." "You'll easily judge," he repeated: you will" (147, original emphasis), and is complimented by Douglas on his acuity (147).

In response to Douglas's question "Isn't anybody going?," asked in "almost the tone of hope," the women in the audience are again specifically mentioned as they vow to stay to hear Douglas's story, though their "departure had been fixed" and was obviously desired. One female auditor asks a question about the object of the governess's affections in anticipation of Douglas's narrative; the narrative "I" intervenes about a point of information he does not have: "'The story will tell,' I took upon myself to reply." The female questioner is then ridiculed as a reader in the following exchange:

> "Oh I can't wait for the story!"
> "The story won't tell," said Douglas; "not in any literal vulgar way."
> "More's the pity then. That's the only way I ever understand." (original emphasis)

It is explicitly the female auditor/reader who is targeted in this way. The narrative "I" clarifies that the manuscript we are reading is "an exact transcript" of the one Douglas read to the group, and celebrates the fact that they got rid of most of the women in the audience before Douglas's reading, further sealing the homosocial exchange of the frame narrative.

> The departing ladies who had said they would stay didn't, of course, thank heaven, stay: they departed, in consequence of arrangements made, in a rage of curiosity, as they professed, produced by the touches with which he had already worked us up. But that only made his little final auditory more compact and select. (148)

This narrator is closely aligned with the author of the novella. When a "lady" in the audience asks Douglas for a title, his reply of "I haven't one" is followed by the frame narrator's exclamation (given in direct speech) "Oh I have!" (original emphasis). Thus the unnamed male "I" narrator is linked to the author of the text we are reading, authorizing its attitude toward the female auditors of Douglas's narrative. The world of the first narrative is a framing patriarchy, following Heidi Hartmann's definition of patriarchy as "relations between men, which have a material base, and which, though hierarchical, establish or create interdependence and solidarity among men that enable them to dominate women" (quoted in Sedgwick 1990: 184).

The contempt for the female audience in the text of the first narrative shapes our reading of the governess's subsequent narrative. The governess's tale presented at/as the heart of this story is preceded by a misogynous exchange and is not followed (supported) by a resumption of the frame narrative. Her isolation at Bly (the novel's setting, where the governess, children, and a skeletal staff are comfortably—but distantly—maintained by the children's uncle) is repeated in the narrative structure of the novella.

The governess describes herself as "a fluttered anxious girl" as she interviews for the job of governess at Bly, and is portrayed as excitable and fanciful from the beginning of her stay there. The word "fancy" recurs frequently in the early part of her narrative, as do other words suggesting her instability. She tells Mrs Grose, for example, that she is "rather easily carried away" (154), and alludes to her attraction to the bachelor uncle on Harley Street, which led her to take the job at Bly. This echoes James's earlier novel, *The Bostonians* (1886), which is told in a similar mimetically objective narrative mode by a narrator who claims to be "[t]he historian who has gathered these documents together" (232). That earlier fiction also asserts a linkage between suggestibility and women: "(they were mainly ladies) whom Selah mesmerized" (66).

Throughout the narrative there are allusions to and images of reading that imply that the governess's perceptions are shaped and distorted by her hyperactive imagination, stimulated by her reading. On her introductory tour of her new home at Bly, led by Flora, one of the two children she was to supervise, she tells us: "I had the view of a castle of romance inhabited by a rosy sprite, such a place as would somehow, for diversion of the young idea, take all color out of storybooks and fairy-tales. Wasn't it just a storybook over which I had fallen a-doze and a-dream?" (155–56). Reader resistance is immediately aroused by the suggestion that fact and fancy may not be sufficiently distinguished in her perceptions. Her fantasies are expressed in reading imagery, "as charming as a charming story" (163). Contrasted to her we have the housekeeper, Mrs. Grose, whom the narrator sees as "a magnificent monument to the blessing of a want of imagination" (202), who never sees the ghosts that the governess later does and who, we are told, is illiterate (158). This opposition reinforces the implication that the governess does not always distinguish between her imagination, informed by her reading, and the external world.

Her first sighting of a ghost is described in terms of a merging of the two ("the sense that my imagination had, in a flash, turned real" [164]), terms that the reader is already prepared to doubt. Her subsequent attempts at interpretation are also given in terms of her reading: "Was there a 'secret' at Bly—a mystery of Udolpho or an insane, an unmentionable relative kept in unsuspected confinement?" (166). These are allusions to two female-authored Gothic novels, *The Mysteries of Udolpho* by Ann Radcliffe and *Jane Eyre* by Charlotte Brontë, which she tells us are "last-century fiction . . . which . . . had reached the sequestered home and appealed to the unavowed curiosity of . . . [her] youth" (194–95). She describes her job as one with "no grey prose," only "the romance of the nursery and the poetry of the schoolroom" (167), and talks of her understanding of her situation after she "had restlessly read into the facts before us almost all the meaning they were to receive from subsequent and more cruel occurrences" (178).

The governess's emotions are also described in extravagant

terms. Waiting to meet Miles, Flora's older brother and the governess's second charge, she describes herself as possessed "of a curiosity that, all the next hours, was to deepen almost to pain" (158).
Having allowed herself to think ill of Miles, whom she had not yet
met, she describes the excessively emotional aftermath when,
"catching my pupil [Flora] in my arms, [the governess] covered her
with kisses in which there was a sob of atonement" (158–59).

Later, talking to Mrs. Grose about her growing understanding of
the ghostly intruders's intentions, she describes her "exaltation"
(176), a word she repeats when describing her feelings about what
she acknowledges as her "obsession" (212). She tells of being "able
to find a joy in the extraordinary flight of heroism the occasion demanded of me" (179). Her aggression toward her friend Mrs. Grose
("It comes back to me that I thought instantly of this as something
I could get from her" [172]; "I shall get it out of you yet!" [190]),
and toward her young charge Flora ("I had never had such a sense
of losing an advantage acquired [the thrill of which had just been
so prodigious]" [197]; "I must have gripped my little girl with a
spasm that, wonderfully, she submitted to" [198]) anticipate the aggression directed toward Miles at the end of the novella, which kills
him. She indirectly admits that her feelings for the children
turned, at some point, to hatred. ("Adorable they must in truth
have been, I now feel, since I didn't in these days hate them!"
[214].)

Her credibility is further impaired when she boasts to her companion Mrs. Grose that, had she been in Mrs. Grose's place, she
would have confronted "the master" with what she knew about
Quint, former servant turned ghost ("I promise you I would have
told!" [177, original emphasis]). This, of course, is exactly what she
fails to do in the present, analogous situation, even after Mrs. Grose
begins to ask her to (208). Reader resistance is aroused when the
governess lies to Mrs. Grose as she elaborates on her encounter
with the ghost of Miss Jessel, her predecessor. The governess
comes upon Miss Jessel in the nursery, sitting at her desk. She describes the ghost as rising "not as if she had heard me" and standing before her. She tells us that Miss Jessel "had looked at me long
enough to appear to say that her right to sit at my table was as good
as mine to sit at hers" (my emphasis), responding to the governess's shout "by looking as if she heard me" and disappearing (221).

Recounting the encounter to Mrs. Grose, the governess tells her that:

". . . I came home . . . for a talk with Miss Jessel." . . . "A talk! Do you mean she spoke?" "It came to that. I found her, on my return, in the schoolroom." "And what did she say?" I can hear the good woman still, and the candour of her stupefaction. "That she suffers the torments—!" It was this, of a truth that made her, as she filled out my picture, gape. "Do you mean," she faltered "—of the lost?" "Of the lost. Of the damned. And that's why, to share them—" I faltered myself with the horror of it. But my companion, with less imagination, kept me up. "To share them—?" "She wants Flora." (223)

At this point the governess's fancy has turned into falsehood and reader resistance to her narrative is heightened. She continues to lie to Mrs. Grose, though this time acknowledging it to the reader. When Mrs. Grose asks her if she has written the children's uncle asking him to come to Bly, she answers in the affirmative, while telling us: "But I didn't add—for the hour—that my letter, sealed and directed, was still in my pocket" (230).

Thus the governess's fancy and ultimate dishonesty combine with her aggressive determination to "get it out of [Miles]" and "save" both children. And so it is that she kills him, aggressively energized by "the effect upon me of an implication of surrender even so faint" (255). She tells us:

My face must have shown him I believed him utterly; yet my hands—but it was for pure tenderness—shook him as if to ask him why, if it was all for nothing, he had condemned me to months of torment. [my emphasis]

He looked in vague pain all round the top of the room and drew his breath, two or three times over, as if with difficulty. . . . He almost smiled at me in the desolation of his surrender, which was indeed practically, by this time, so complete that I ought to have left it there. But I was infatuated—I was blind with victory, though even then the very effect that was to have brought him so much nearer was already that of added separation. (259)

My sternness . . . made him avert himself again, and that movement made me, with a single bound and an irrepressible cry, spring straight upon him. (260, original emphasis)

At this, after a second in which his head made the movement of a baf-
fled dog's on a scent and then gave a frantic little shake for air and light
. . . he had already jerked straight round, stared, glared again, and seen
but the quiet day. With the stroke of the loss I was so proud of he ut-
tered the cry of a creature hurled over an abyss, and the grasp with
which I recovered him might have been that of catching him in his fall
. . . his little heart, dispossessed, had stopped. (261–62)

Reading the governess's narrative in isolation, without attention to
the introductory narrative, produces a different text. That isolated
text has led critics to argue over questions of hysteria, the supernat-
ural, or ultimate ambiguity. Reading the governess's narrative
through the fissures of its framing and narrative crossings shifts the
ground of interpretation.

James's preface to *The Turn of the Screw* reflects his attempt to
use the author-function to prevent what Foucault calls "the prolif-
eration of meaning" (1980: 209). James claims for his text "the
small strength . . . of a perfect homogeneity, of being . . . all of a
kind" (35), whose "aim [was] at an absolute singleness, clearness
and roundness, and yet to depend on an imagination working
freely" (38). This aim—homogeneity and singleness—is consistent
with what Wolfgang Iser calls "good continuation" (1978: 186),
which does not make great demands on the reader's imagination.
The free-playing imagination of the preface must then be that of
the author. His text is seemingly a heteroglossic text in that it
allows for speaking voices other than the author's. However, the
author's presence as arbiter of meaning is established from the beginning of the tale in the narrative "I," which forms an identity
with the author by bringing us the manuscript which he has enti-
tled. (The narrator's response to Douglas's lack of a title for the governess's manuscript, "Oh I have!," invites the reader to conflate
the narrator with the author of the titled manuscript of the governess's narrative in hand.)

The misogynous exchange in the introductory narrative and the
hierarchy of the layered narrative structure shape the reading of the
governess's narrative. This double-yet-open-framed, multivoiced
text silences or ridicules the female voices of its first narrative while
leaving the gender-marked narrator of its central narrative alone
with her ghosts. The ideology of *The Turn of the Screw* can be found
in its reification ("representing a transitory, historical state of affairs

as if it were permanent, natural, outside of time" [Thompson 1984: 130]), as we can see if we attend to its context.

If we return it to its *fin de siècle* origin, we can see that the novel reflects the ambivalence of nineteenth-century medical practitioners toward hysterics. Carroll Smith-Rosenberg's short history describes the hysteric's "passive aggression" (1972: 671) and the perception of both medical practitioners and patients in the nineteenth century that hysteria was "both peculiarly female and peculiarly sexual" (669). The disease provoked "ambivalence and in many cases . . . hostility" in the male physicians and family members confronted by it (671). Biographical implications are not my focus here, though they are also interesting in the context of James's relationship with his invalid sister Alice. Situating *The Turn of the Screw* in the context of its production also places it within what Elaine Showalter describes as the feminization of hysteria in nineteenth-century medical discourse (1985). She cites the observation of late-nineteenth-century doctors that "hysterical patients were likely to be more independent and assertive than 'normal' women, 'exhibiting more than usual force and decision of character, of strong resolution, fearless of danger'" (145, original emphasis). Showalter also quotes Octavia Wilberforce, a physician who, in about 1920, at the beginning of her career, worked briefly at a mental institution where

> [s]he observed that many [of the patients] were former governesses. "Why should teaching send you dotty? Continual hard work, no future, no ambitions, bad pay, eh?" The worst cases seemed to be "the inelastic conservative governesses in military families"; and Wilberforce quickly perceived the connection between women's economic dependence and oppression, and mental breakdown. (201–202, original emphasis)

The perception by this female doctor of a socioeconomic link to mental illness is totally absent in the perceptions of male doctors working only twenty years earlier, contemporaries of James. At this diagnostic juncture, James's novel embraces both directions of thought, contemporary and anticipatory. Reading the novella through the fissures of its choices of narrative mode and frame, we see that it is less ambiguous and more ambidextrous. The narrative structure of *The Turn of the Screw* reflects both late-nineteenth-century discourse on hysteria and James's ambivalence toward it, giving the governess voice while concomitantly provoking reader resistance to that voice.

3

On Heteroglossia

Cries and tears: an aphasic enunciation of what appears without one's knowing where it came from (from what obscure debt or writing of the body), without one's knowing how it could be said except through the other's voice.

—de Certeau (1984: 163)

THE PREVIOUS TWO CHAPTERS LOOKED AT THE COUPLED FISSURES OF narrative cross-gendering and prefatory or framing narratives. Their shared focus is on ways the reader is positioned at the beginning of the reading experience, and how that positioning sets up subsequent interactions with the text's narrative mode. Following the mimetic structure of Part I on its axis of the reading experience, this chapter moves from textual beginning to body. The fissure of cross-gendered narration continues to be read here (it is a constant of Part I), coupled with fissures of multivoiced narratives, textual heteroglossia. Thus the shift in focus is also one of voice. Chapters 1 and 2 looked at texts that use serial first-person narration to introduce and add textual voices. The texts of this chapter are twentieth-century mimetic fictions that use cross-gendered narration within heteroglossic narratives, expanding the choral potential of texts and allowing us to listen to ways in which complicity and resistance are elicited in response to textual voices. In his useful neologism (which has taken its place in the language of critical reading), Mikhail Bakhtin defines heteroglossia in the novel as

a special type of double-voiced discourse [which] . . . serves two speakers at the same time and expresses simultaneously two different intentions: the direct intention of the character who is speaking, and the refracted intention of the author. In such discourse there are two voices, two meanings and two expressions. And all the while these two voices are dialogically interrelated, they—as it were—know about each

54

other (just as two exchanges in a dialogue know of each other and are structured in this mutual knowledge of each other); it is as if they actually hold a conversation with each other. (1981: 324)

The texts of this chapter approach the Bakhtinian ideal of the heteroglossic novel, engaging voices of South Africa at a transitional moment of its history, mediated by marginalized narrators who elicit both complicity and resistance from their readers.

In *The Practice of Everyday Life* (1984), Michel de Certeau describes an "immense field" of narratives that he calls "heterologies" that "have the common characteristic of attempting to write the voice" (149, original emphasis). He sees these heterologies as "a point of departure for so many 'life stories'" (159), multivoiced narratives whose written form contains traces of oral predecessors. This heterological literature

> tells both what it does with orality (it alters it) and it remains altered with and by the voice. Texts thus express an altered voice in the writing the voice makes necessary by its insurmountable difference. In this literature, we have thus a first image of the voice simultaneously "cited" (as before a court of law) and "altered"—a lost voice, erased even within the object itself (the "fable") whose scriptural construction it makes possible. (de Certeau: 161)

I view heterological literature's vocal multiplicity as its primary fissure, a narrative strategy that signals its reader to attend to the multivoiced potential of the text and to interpret it. Heterological literature instigated by first-person narration functions similarly to de Certeau's description of citation: "[T]he ultimate weapon for making people believe . . . ; it is the means by which the 'real' is instituted" (188). The direct speech of citation and that of first-person narration are central tools of mimetic fiction.

Narrative mode is one of the "markers within [texts] of historical situation" (Chambers 1984: 10). This chapter looks at multiplicity of voices in two 1990 novels by South African authors writing about their society in transition, Nadine Gordimer's *My Son's Story* and J. M. Coetzee's *Age of Iron*. Both are heterologies, in the coinage of de Certeau, using cross-gendered narration together with other-voiced texts to view a society where large numbers of the population are just beginning to gain a public voice. Reflecting this historical moment, private and public voices engage the reader in concomitant complicity and resistance, echoing the extremity and the potential of this moment of transition.

In *My Son's Story* Nadine Gordimer crosses in "reverse passing" as she creates the voice of an adolescent mixed-race boy narrating her novel of South Africa at an historic crossroads, crossing race, gender, and generation. By the end of the twentieth century, it is youth, not gender, that Gordimer uses to position her narrator on the margins of the society he is reporting on. This female-authored "reverse passing" thus serves the same function that male-authored cross-gendering served in earlier fiction. It creates a narrative point of view at the margins of a society that enables the narrator to observe and comment on that society while being absolved of responsibility for changing it, a position no longer automatically female in late-twentieth-century Western societies. Similarly due to changing gender roles in these societies, Nadine Gordimer's cross-gendering reflects a shift in female-authored cross-gendered narratives as women writers no longer need to gain a normative position relative to the society they are writing about by assuming a male voice.

For Nadine Gordimer writing about South Africa struggling toward historic change, gender-crossing is one narrative strategy adopted in a heterglossic narrative that is told partly by an adolescent boy and partly by a third-person narrator focalizing through various characters (embedding free indirect and free direct discourse in the narration), with direct speech in the voices of all the characters. ("Free" discourse is unmarked. In direct speech, this means that there are no quotation marks; in indirect speech, no markers such as "he answered that. . . .") Gordimer's novel achieves the egalitarian polyphony envisioned for the novel as a genre by Bakhtin. In this vision of the novel's potential, Bakhtin writes: "the novel must represent all the social and ideological voices of its era . . . the novel must be a microcosm of heteroglossia . . . one single heteroglot unit of social becoming. Every language in the novel is a point of view, a socio-ideological conceptual system of real social groups and their embodied representatives." (1981: 411).

My Son's Story (1990) realizes this Bakhtinian ideal of the heteroglossic novel in several ways. Its multiple perspective is anticipated in the title of the novel, whose possessives remain ambiguous. Will, the young narrator (named by his father for William Shakespeare), writes his first manuscript, the novel that we read. In the final sentence of her narrator's manuscript, Gordimer points to her act of ventriloquism in what is also the final sentence of her book, as Will declares of the text we have just finished reading: "I am a writer and this is my first book—that I can never publish" (277). He writes, he tells us, because he "was excluded" from political action but remains "the one to record . . . what he [Will's father Sonny] and my mother/Aila and Baby [Will's sister] and the others did, what it really was like to live a life determined by the struggle to be free" (276).

Clearly then it is not Will's voice that we hear in the title of the story he claims he is telling us. Perhaps this is Sonny, Will's father, speaking the title. Or perhaps Sonny (whose name, "the generic diminutive by which they had celebrated him as the son [original emphasis], the first-born male, was to stay with him in the changing identities a man passes through, for the rest of his life" [5] is the son of the title, the speaking voice being that of his father, Will's grandfather, one of the unwritten generations of mixed-race and black South Africans whose stories were never recorded, whose "oral family history had gone to the grave" (5). Or perhaps this is Aila's voice, the narrator's mother, whose gender roles (spousal, maternal) veil her political involvement from her son and storyteller for much of the novel. The ambiguity of the possessives of the title—whose son and whose story—reflects the shifting identities and political climate of the South Africa of the novel.

The connection between son and story is also introduced in the epigraph to the novel, the last line of Shakespeare's Sonnet 13 ("You had a father—let your son say so"), a sonnet aimed at persuading the poem's addressee to have a son as a hedge against the absoluteness of death. It is a connection that the novel makes explicitly political in repeated and varied modes. The personal and the political and their representation in narrative are contemplated from several points of view. From Sonny's point of view, in free direct speech embedded in third-person narration, we hear his political evolution reflected in his musing about himself as "prisoner of conscience": "you sit in detention, on trial, convicted for the liberty of all your people. That conscience takes precedence over any conscience about a wife and family left to shift for themselves, and over any woman you have need of" (p. 157).

Hannah, Sonny's lover and the woman "you have need of" of his thoughts, expresses a similar opinion in embedded discourse that moves from free indirect to free direct speech: "But between them, that wasn't possible; you don't live for each other, the loving is contained within the cause, and there would be no love if you were to refuse, because of personal risk, something expected of you by the struggle" (174). The third-person narrator also insists on the connection between individual lives and power politics. Describing Hannah's history, the narrator sums it up as "[a]n individual life, Hannah's, but one that has followed the shifts in power of the communities into which she was born" (87). And Will, the first-person narrator of the novel, makes the connection between the personal and the political, families and politics, through frequent references to Shakespeare's *King Lear* and *Hamlet* and, of course, in his final declaration of purpose: "to record what [his family] and the others did, what it really was like to live a life determined by the struggle to be free" (276).

My Son's Story is several stories of political education and evolution, a multifocused *Bildungsroman* representing the *Bildung* of South Africa as it struggles free of racial oppression and apartheid. Each of the characters moves toward resistance in the course of the novel; only Will, the narrator who grows from early adolescence to young manhood in the novel, remains outside the circles of active resistance. His *Bildung* is measured in terms of his uneasy self-fashioning as, through learning to see his mother, he moves toward a clearer vision of his society, an understanding that transcends the division between colored and black to which he initially adheres. The heteroglossic text of the novel subverts Will's claim of "knowing them [the other characters] too well" as it reveals his misreadings and misunderstandings. Foremost among these is his mother's story.

Aila's point of view is initially presented in juxtaposition with (and therefore possibly as sharing) the universal "colored" point of view, one that allows her family a place above the bottom of the social ladder. When her husband is fired from his teaching job for leading the children at his colored school to join black children in a demonstration, this point of view is presented within the narration in free indirect discourse. "No wonder parents wanted removed from the school a teacher, one of their own kind, who led their children over there" (28). This colored point of view is given voice early in the novel as one measure of the political growth represented through the various characters. The hierarchies imposed by whites are perpetuated by mixed-race people, who perceive their interests in conflict with those of blacks and who must learn to see this as collaboration in their own oppression.

> The blacks . . . went back to their own areas when the work was done. . . . Better that way. . . . [I]t was because of <u>them</u> that the school-teacher's community was what it was: cast outside the town. Needing uplift. It was because of <u>them</u> whose pigment darkened the blood, pro-created a murky dilution in the veins of the white town, disowned by the white town, that the community was disqualified by the white town, that the community was disqualified for the birthright of the cinema, the library, the lavatories . . . With that strain of pigment went more interdictions. . . . Better to keep them at a distance, not recognize any feature in them. And yet they were useful . . . beneath your station; for nothing was beneath theirs. (22, original emphasis)

Both Will and Sonny fail to notice Aila's political activity. For Will, Aila's role as his mother blinds him to any possibility of change in her; for Sonny, "Poor Aila," discarded wife, is stuck in values that he has long outgrown. Both son and father fail to interpret the in-formation that they have, blinded as they are by Aila's role as "stay-at-home wife—and mother" (147); she is inconceivable as a revolutionary. They see what they "expected of her" (168), and not what she has become. Noticing that his mother takes frequent flights to visit her daughter and grandson in Lusaka and assuming her to be on unpaid leave, Will doesn't question the source of her travel money, since Aila "is used to managing with little money, she doesn't skimp us, in the household, and yet apparently she is able to save enough for airfares" (177). Will even notices his mother deceiving him as to her destination as he drops her off on an er-rand, yet he can only interpret her lie as pathetically manipulative of himself (187). The telephone rings with long-distance calls for Aila, and Will can only see her as his "poor mother . . . and her brave show of having a life of her own" (197). He patronizes her, and at the thought that she might have a secret life or love, he de-clares himself "old enough, now, almost to wish it were true" (197).

Even after Aila is arrested for concealing explosives in the store-room of their home, father and son fail to see her. Her husband Sonny cannot see around his own shadow, sure that the explosives were planted by the police as a "frame-up to trap him" (218). In the space of a few sentences, her son Will first blames his sister for manipulating his mother into this dangerous situation, and then taunts his father for thinking the same thing ("he was mistaken in his demeaning decision . . . that she was manipulated, beguiled into use by Baby [her daughter] and that husband" [232]). It is only at her trial that they finally see "her hidden face [and] . . . recognize her" (230). This recognition is signaled by Will in a distinction between the person he now calls Aila and that of his mother, "that exemplary wife and home-maker whose retiring nature and virtues as a conscientious worker were attested to by the highly-respected medical practitioner by whom she had been employed for years" (233). Even Sonny moves from seeing her as "Poor Aila" to recognizing her as "Aila a revolutionary responsible for her acts" (239). And since this political drama is deeply interwoven with the family drama, Sonny's passion for his wife, long spent, is revived by this recognition of her, and erstwhile "Poor Aila," now revolutionary, again becomes "his wife, his Aila" (242). The political and the personal remain inseparable. As this family disintegrates, the narrator focalizes through Sonny, speculating on the origin of the change in Aila. "Perhaps he flattered himself Aila had needed to suffer his love of another woman to change. Perhaps it had nothing to do with that, with him. Perhaps she had freed herself just as he had, through the political struggle" (258).

The limited vision of the shifting narrative modes of the novel provokes reader resistance, fissures emphasizing both the impossibility of certainty of knowledge of the kind Will claims to possess and the possibility of growth through seeing and telling. Will gets a message from Aila through a young black woman and feels proud of his people, asserting that "Whites don't know what they're seeing when they look at us [and] . . . I want to tell them" (261). The process of self-becoming is what the narrative heteroglossia enacts, as the reader is encouraged to follow this complex multi-voiced narrative of a society in the process of struggle, recognition and change. In *My Son's Story*, Gordimer realizes the Bakhtinian ideal of the novel as "one single heteroglot unit of social becoming" (1981: 411) in her polyphonic fictional narrative of South Africa struggling toward an historic crossroads. No longer bound by cultural gender roles in the way that her nineteenth-century predecessors were, Gordimer's narrative strategy of cross-gendering

threaded throughout by direct and indirect speech of other characters becomes homologous with the shifts and crossings that produced and sustain society in present-day South Africa.

J. M. Coetzee's similarly heterologic novel *Age of Iron* (1990) offers
an interesting gloss on Nadine Gordimer's contemporaneous novel
of the same society. His narrative strategy of "reverse passing" both
follows that of earlier male-authored crossed-gendered narratives
and alters it. Male-authored cross-gendering in twentieth-century
Western literature reflects both changes in cultural gender concepts and the continuing dominance of patriarchal structures.
Gender-crossing is no longer necessarily an enactment of what Goffman calls "reverse passing," "concealment of creditable facts" (in
this case, masculine gender) in society (Goffman 1970: 58), and
this reflects changes in attitudes toward gender in Western society.
However, gender-crossing for male authors retains its reverse-pass-
ing potential in a way that no longer holds for the passing-potential
of twentieth-century female-authored gender-crossings. In other
words, while contemporary female authors no longer need cross-
gendering to achieve a normative position relative to society, the
persistently patriarchal foundations of Western society still allow
contemporary male authors to use cross-gendering to position
themselves on the margin of the society they are describing, particularly if the focus of their narrative is social. Elizabeth Harvey's observation about gender-crossing in Renaissance literature remains
true for much contemporary male-authored literature. Harvey interprets cross-gendering as a strategy of literary production "in
which woman stands as the silent but enabling condition of writing" (1992: 78). She argues that gender-crossing (which she terms
transvestite ventriloquism) in Renaissance literature "is an appropriation of the feminine voice, and that it reflects and contributes
to a larger cultural silencing of women. . . . [Thus the issue] is not
whether male poets can adequately represent the female voice, but
the ethics and politics of doing so" (12). Cross-gendering in male-
authored twentieth-century narrative fiction retains its potential
for marginal positioning in these still patriarchal societies.

The interesting difference in Coetzee's late-twentieth-century
novel is a reflection of changing gender roles in Western societies:
The author cannot gain a position of marginality merely by speaking as a woman. Marginality in Western societies at the end of the

twentieth century is no longer automatically feminized; thus Coetzee's narrator is a woman dying of cancer, her illness together with
her gender positioning her as observer rather than participant. Indeed, her twofold marginality takes precedence over her other significant identity as an enfranchised member of the ruling white
supremacist minority. The narrator is in South Africa, writing her
dying reflections to her daughter, who left South Africa years earlier for a new life in North America, in a manuscript to be mailed
after her death. As in Gordimer's novel, the personal and the political are inextricably intertwined. As the narrator writes of her fears
about the unreliability of the alcoholic derelict upon whom she depends to mail her manuscript to her daughter after her death, with
her daughter consequently possibly never even knowing of the existence of these writings, she declares her view that this writing is
"[a] certain body of truth . . .: my truth: how I lived in these times,
in this place" (119). Time and place are meticulously described in
this portrait of South Africa in the final throes of apartheid.

Improved vision is both what is represented in *Age of Iron* and
what is enacted as part of the process of reader response in this
novel, as it is in *My Son's Story*. Looking at a photograph of her
infant self in the garden with her mother and brother, the aged narrator tries to see past the margins of the photograph, to see what
she had not seen at the time. She looks for those "outside the picture, leaning on their rakes, leaning on their spades, waiting to get
back to work, lean[ing] also against the edge of the rectangle, bend-
ing it, bursting it in" (102). The narrator goes on to describe the
changes in South Africa in terms of this movement of the margin
to the center.

> No longer does the picture show who were in the garden frame that
> day, but who were not there. Lying all these years in places of safekeep-
> ing across the country, in albums, in desk drawers, this picture and
> thousands like it have subtly matured, metamorphosed. The fixing did
> not hold or the developing went further than one would ever have
> dreamed—who can know how it happened?—but they have become
> negatives again, a new kind of negative in which we begin to see what
> used to lie outside the frame, occulted. (102–103)

Having carefully positioned his narrator on the margins of the dis-
integrating society he is representing in the novel, Coetzee has her

offer us a vision of what there is to see in this shifting political landscape. Margins and center are no longer stable, as this metaphor of
the photograph overstepping its frame illustrates. Coetzee's narrator, centrally situated in the old photograph, observes this shifting
landscape from the marginality of her invalid subject position, a position that invites reader complicity.

But reader complicity invited in response to the narrator's subject position is qualified by inherent limitations of vision and language. The impossibility of fully or truthfully representing this
society in language is insisted on by the narrator. In direct speech
to a black crowd in the wasteland of a burning ghetto, she acknowledges the poverty of her articulated response. One of the crowd dis-
misses her with the remark that she "talks shit," an evaluation that
she accepts while also accepting the impossibility of any alternative.

> "But what do you expect?" I went on. "To speak of this"—I waved a
> hand over the bush, the smoke, the filth littering the path—"you would
> need the tongue of a god." (91)

Why does the narrator claim that one "would need the tongue of
a god" to describe this desolation? She offers an explanation of
sorts early in the novel (her testimony to her daughter, "[s]ix pages
already" [8]), where she conflates word and body in describing her
manuscript as an embodied narrative. Here the narrator describes
her writing as a process where "day by day I render myself into
words and pack the words into the page like sweets: like sweets for
my daughter, for her birthday, for the day of her birth. Words out
of my body, drops of myself, for her to unpack in her own time, to
take in, to suck, to absorb" (8).

These embodied words contain both writer and the written object, and it is perhaps this Christian view of sacrificial exchange
that explains the narrator's later observation that such a history
could only be told by a god. In this novel, the terminally ill woman
narrator is the closest position to this godlike perch, with the narrator given the detachment of approaching death in a yet embodied
character. Incorporating into herself the object of her writing—the
alcoholic derelict upon whom she depends to mail her manuscript
after her death—she explains that she writes of him "because he is
and is not I. Because in the look he gives me I see myself in a way
that can be written. . . . When I write about him I write about my-

self. When I write about his dog I write about myself; when I write about the house I write about myself" (8).

The narrator insists that these conflations of words and body and writer and written are the outcome of a particular historical moment ("in this world, in this time" [8]), one of acute political and social significance. Through the narrator's views on the narrative necessities and historical specificity of the moment of writing, Coetzee encodes instructions to his reader to resist the voices in his text, despite the authenticity suggested by the metaphors of empathy and the self-ironic admissions of limitation. In other words, these very self-reflexive moments in the narrative invite reader resistance because they remind the reader of the contingencies and limitations of the narrator's point of view, and emphasize the impossibility of attaining the godlike perspective that the narrator insists upon.

Dialogically present in his narrator's voice, thereby, Coetzee has her articulate both the resistance that his narrative mode invites and its rationale. Directly addressing her daughter, she urges skepticism even toward her own dying words, a skepticism demanded by the historical and political situation of the moment of writing ("in this world, in this time" [8]), and by the pain and suffering of the dead and homeless that must be seen through her own pain and suffering:

> I tell you the story of this morning mindful that the storyteller, from her office, claims the place of right. It is through my eyes that you see; the voice that speaks in your head is mine. Through me alone do you find yourself here on these desolate flats, smell the smoke in the air, see the bodies of the dead, hear the weeping, shiver in the rain. . . .
>
> Now, my child, flesh of my flesh, my best self, I ask you to draw back: attend to the writing, not to me. If lies and pleas and excuses weave among the words, listen for them. Do not pass them over, do not forgive them easily. Read them all, even this adjuration, with a cold eye. . . .
>
> Do not read in sympathy with me. Let your heart not beat with mine. (95–96)

These instructions of narrator to narratee (to "learn how things are" by attending to how they are told) are also those of the implied author to the implied reader of the text. This is a demand for an active reading that "provokes the reader constantly to supplement what he is reading" in order to "bring about an intensified participation that will compel the reader to be that much more aware of the intention of the text" (Iser 1989: 22). This type of text creates a resisting and critical reader, and both Gordimer's and Coetzee's contemporaneous cross-gendered South African novels are texts of this kind. These texts also insist on foregrounding the ethical dimension of how one reads and writes. In addition, both reflect changing gender roles in Western societies in their narrative modes, as their gender crossings aim for a marginal position of the narrator as observer, a position no longer inherently gendered, but determined as well by youth, ethnicity, invalidism. And finally, both novels' narrative strategies using cross-gendered narrators of limited vision through which other voices are heard realize Bakhtin's egalitarian view of the multivoiced possibilities of the novel genre, and de Certeau's hope of the recovery of at least traces of lost and muted voices.

While necessarily falling short of Bakhtin's reach (to "represent *all* the social and ideological voices of its era"), the plurivocal narratives of *My Son's Story* and *Age of Iron* enact the "social becoming" of late-twentieth-century South Africa, which is both their shared setting and theme.

4

On Temporary and Permanent Gaps

STORYTELLING NECESSITATES SELECTION, THE FOCUS OF THIS CHAPTER. The key fissure of temporary and permanent gaps is coupled here with the constant of Part I—the fissure of cross-gendered narration—to bring the process of selection into view. In the series of events that form a narrative, it is often revealing to note untold events and to ask the question that drives all interpretation: "to what end?" In previous chapters we have asked what is served by authorial choices about framing and voicing narratives; attending to textual delays, exclusions, and silences can be similarly exegetically rewarding. Temporary and permanent gaps[1] are particularly salient in this regard.

The method here is similar to working a puzzle. The puzzle pieces located within the frame both disclose the information they contain and outline the adjacent missing pieces. Authorial decisions to leave pieces temporarily or permanently missing can be hermeneutically significant or trivial. Attending to them is an important part of the process of critical reading. This chapter takes its place at the end of the mimetically structured Part I, focusing on the end of the reading experience through looking at the coupled fissures of cross-gendered narration and gaps.

Three male-authored female-narrated narratives of different periods and cultural contexts that share a central gap of mothers abandoning their children offer a rich field for looking at the effects of gaps on reader response. *A Yellow Raft in Blue Water* (Michael Dorris, 1987), *Kate Vaiden* (Reynolds Price, 1986), and *Moll Flanders* (Daniel Defoe, 1722) offer an interesting look at the narrative fissure of temporary and permanent gaps in three very different societies. Through them we can also see an evolution in male-authored cross-gendered fiction in the move from social to psychosocial mimesis, from Goffman's reverse passing engendering

Englisches Seminar
Universität Basel
Nadelberg 6
CH-4051 Basel
Tel. 061/261 26 81

reader complicity (in eighteenth-century *Moll Flanders*) to a Bakhtinian dialogism eliciting concomitant complicity and resistance (in
twentieth-century *A Yellow Raft in Blue Water* and *Kate Vaiden*).
Both fissures (cross-gendering and gaps), and their effect on reader
response to narrative voice, reflect this change.

The gaps in the accounts of the lives of Christine, Kate, and Moll
surround their abandonment of their children. In *A Yellow Raft*, the
gap is temporary, a function of the limited view of first-person narration that is progressively resolved in a serial narrative spanning
three generations of mother-daughter relations. In *Kate Vaiden* the
gap seems temporary (with motive for abandonment given at the
novel's end), while in effect it is permanent, with the gap inade-
quately filled (as I argue in this chapter). Kate gives several con-
vincing reasons for leaving her loved ones, yet when she is
attempting to account for thirty-five years of staying away, the gaps
in the narrative are not persuasive, unintentionally creating reader
resistance in a novel dependent on complicity. This fissure, in a
text dependent on psychosocial mimesis, undermines the novel. In
Moll Flanders the gap is permanent, tolerated—even unnoticed—by the reader because of the novel's socially (not psychosocially) mimetic genre. Moll's narrative is vague in accounting for
(and in the counting of) her children, yet because of the social realism that is the intention of the text, this vagueness does not under-
mine the authority of the novel's narrative voice.

ON TEMPORARY GAPS

Michael Dorris's *A Yellow Raft in Blue Water* (1987) combines
techniques we have seen in earlier narratives, affording a look at
familiar fissures differently joined while adding the fissure of temporary gaps. The novel uses three cross-gendered narratives (as
does Mary Shelley in *Frankenstein*), serially (as Henry James does
in *Turn of the Screw*) not concentrically (as in Shelley's novel). And
Dorris's three serially presented cross-gendered narratives are
punctuated throughout by the direct speech of various characters
(which neither Shelley nor James do), giving voice to the many "in-
finitely obscure lives [that] remain to be recorded" (Woolf: 89).

A Yellow Raft in Blue Water is a novel narrated in the first-person
by a mother who abandons her child. Dorris places two first-person

narratives on either side of the abandoning mother's, beginning his novel with the abandoned daughter's narrative and ending it with that of the child's grandmother. Narrated in three voices, crossing gender and generations, this novel tells the stories of three Native American women: a teenage daughter, Rayona; her middle-aged mother, Christine; and her grandmother, Ida. Through these crossings and through frequent use of the direct speech of other characters embedded in the three narratives, Dorris shows us Native American society, both rural and urban. He traces this society through the divisive Vietnam War (162–70) and the following decade, through the evolution of the reservation into a "nation" and the Indian into a "Native American" (159), with the changed self-perception to which these linguistic changes attest.

Dorris tells his story through the consciousness of three very differently positioned women in a novel of abundant quotation, the direct speech of its other characters. This strategy of punctuated multiple narration allows the novel to represent and enact—compelling its reader also to enact—its main concern: the perception and comprehension of the Other, both across and within cultures and among and within families. This main theme also necessitates the temporary nature of the aforementioned gap, with Christine's motive for leaving her child (Christine's terminal illness) resolved and justified within the narrative itself (the motive consonant with characterization). Dorris's temporary gap provides suspense and propels the novel, yet its transience ensures that his reader is not distracted by unresolved aspects of a central theme. *A Yellow Raft in Blue Water* realizes the Bakhtinian ideal of a multivoiced representation of "real social groups and their embodied representatives," the "social and ideological voices of its era" (1981: 411). Dorris's gender-and-generation narrative crossings combine with the direct speech of the other characters in this novel to represent late twentieth-century Native American society.

It is the final sentence of the novel that summarizes its narrative strategy and situates both implied reader and implied author (the textual markers of intended audience and authorial presence) in a cross-cultural exchange that necessarily involves the miscomprehensions inherent in cultural crossings. Ida, the elderly narrator given the last section of the novel, remembers an evening sitting outside her home on the reservation, accompanied by the mission priest, Father Hurlburt. In the dark rural night, he cannot see what she is doing with her lifted arms, and so he asks her for an explanation. Ending her narrative and Dorris's novel with the following words, Ida tells us that Father Hurlburt, "[a]s a man with cut hair, . . . did not identify the rhythm of three strands, the whispers of coming and going, of twisting and tying and blending, of catching and of letting go, of braiding" (372).

Hurlburt, an elderly man who has lived and worked on the reservation for most of his life (and all of the novel), who has made a successful effort to learn the local language (321), and who is even part Indian (322), remains "a man with cut hair," one whose cultural otherness, in spite of the exposure of a lifetime, makes him unable to comprehend what he sees. Here, I believe, we find the presence of the implied author of the novel, sharing narrative morphology with an image central to Ida and to her people and, through this image, shaping our final view of his braided, three-strand narrative while warning the reader of the potential failures of comprehension inherent in our otherness.

The first strand of the narrative is told by Rayona, the teenage daughter of a single mother, Christine. Christine escapes from a hospital bed in Seattle and drives to the reservation in Montana where she grew up and where, at her childhood home, she abandons Rayona to Rayona's grandmother, Ida. Through a series of chance events, Rayona leaves Ida's home and spends the summer working at a nearby national park, finding her mother again only at the end of the summer. Her narrative is both an account of that summer and an attempt to understand her mother's behavior, which becomes comprehensible only when she is able to face the gravity of her mother's potentially fatal illness, which has triggered Christine's attempt to resituate her daughter as she faces her own impending death.

The voice of teenage Rayona tells this history in the present simple tense, with the voices of other characters embedded in her narrative in direct speech. Selection of tense is one of the primary methods through which Dorris creates the voices of these three distinctly different generations. While teenage Rayona tells her story entirely in the present simple tense, middle-aged Christine narrates hers in the traditional past simple of the retrospective narrative, and elderly but enduring Ida begins her narrative in the present and shifts to the past as she reviews her life from its first major turning point, when she was fifteen, Rayona's age in the novel's present. All three narratives have the voices of all the other characters embedded in their narratives in direct speech.

Misapprehension and misperception are not restricted in the novel to white missionaries. One of the effects of this triple-voiced narrative is to give us different perspectives on the same events and on their histories, thus revealing the limited understanding or access of the characters to those events and histories while gradually expanding the understanding of the reader. For example, Rayona's narrative, which opens the novel, gives us the story of the origin of her grandmother's name, Aunt Ida. She gives us this history as she received it: the appellation came about in response to Ida's discomfort at being an unwed mother when she gave birth to Christine (26). It is only when we reach Ida's narrative that we see that this received history is false, and that Ida's father and her aunt Clara are Christine's biological parents. In other words, Christine is Ida's half-sister or, viewed differently (from the maternal perspective), Ida's first cousin—not her daughter, as both Christine (144) and Rayona (and most of the reservation) assume. In Ida's account, we learn that she had Christine call her "Aunt Ida" as a way of protecting herself and diminishing her attachment to her adopted child in case Ida's aunt Clara, Christine's biological mother, returned to claim the child (325).

Similarly (though with less certainty), Rayona tells us of her belief that her grandmother's claim to have been in Denver is a story invented by Ida "to seem important, to seem as though she belongs to this big church in Colorado" (37). Late in the novel, in Ida's narrative, we hear how she accompanied her aunt Clara to a convent in Denver, Colorado, where Clara gave birth to Christine and from which Ida returned alone with Christine, letting the reservation believe the child was hers (314–23). Thus the narrative layering of the novel forces its reader to misperceive and subsequently to correct her/his perceptions while concomitantly encouraging reader complicity, since each of the narrator's autonomous narratives appears reliable. The narrators tell all they know, but taken together the gaps in their knowledge become perceptible to the reader. It is only the juxtaposition of the narratives and their completed presentation that enable the reader's perception to exceed that of any single character. This limited perception includes that of the elderly Ida, whose history has encompassed them all, and who asserts her belief that "No one but me carries it all [the family history] and no one will—unless I tell Rayona, who might understand" (297). And of course, this assertion of intrinsic limits in the understanding of her potential auditor is yet another representation of the novel's concern with the difficulties of mutual understanding.

The character-narrators are repeatedly misperceived or misunderstood, just as they frequently misperceive or misunderstand, as the novel represents the limitations of perception inevitable in human interaction. Rayona, daughter of a Native American mother and an African-American father, meets her peers on the reservation and "know[s] what they see. Wrong color, outsider, skinny, friend of the priest, friend of the dork" (43). The direct speech of her peers confirms the accuracy of this perception—that is indeed how they view Rayona. The reader, on the foundation of the preceding narrative, knows how profoundly the reservation kids have misperceived Rayona.

Misperception and lack of comprehension are represented in the novel as components of all human relations. As Christine says in her narrative, "You had to have lived my life to understand it" (242). Rayona misunderstands her mother, who comes to retrieve medication in Rayona's absence, a fact that Rayona views as proof that she was "not as important as some package" her mother needed (53). Christine's subsequent narrative exposes the falsity of Rayona's assumption, which the reader temporarily shares, and which is based on a mistaken underestimation of both the gravity of Christine's illness and the depth of her attachment to her child. Both Rayona and Christine mistake each other, as the reader is invited to see early in the novel. In the scene of Christine's escape from hospital, Rayona catches Christine breaking into her own car and thinks she's caught a thief ("some teen [hospital] volunteer" [10]); Christine, caught breaking into her car, mistakes Rayona for a male assailant (241). And fifteen-year-old Ida's misperception of her aunt Clara (298–319) was to determine the rest of her life, resulting in Ida's adoption of Christine and appearance in the reservation as an unwed mother.

Thus, the many voices of this novel, narrated and quoted, enact its thematic interests both in the representation of the twentieth-century Native American community and in the novel's representation of the failures of understanding and empathy inevitable in all human interaction. The braid of the novel's final sentence leaves the reader an image of the braided lives homologously reflected in the braid of the novel's narrative structure, itself a symbol of the Native American male. At the novel's end, this braid is also a braid of the hair that Ida's teenage daughter Christine has unsuccessfully attempted to curl with a home permanent. Braiding, the final image of the novel, literally its last word, is also the novel's final instruction to the reader—to braid the narratives together—and a reflection too of the experience of reading *A Yellow Raft in Blue Water*.

Narrative crossings of the sort demonstrated in this novel (genderic and generational), punctuated by the quoted speech of other characters, are what I have termed fissures, examples of "the response-inviting structures of the text," only some of which are selected by "the actual reader . . . from the potential inherent in the text" (Iser 1989: 50). Gaps function similarly in activating the reader, their response-inducing effect perhaps more insistent—and more visible—than other fissures. Temporary gaps resolved in the course of a narrative are plot-related devices propelling reading with only transitory hermeneutic effect. Engaged page-turning is the activity instigated by temporary gaps.

Reynolds Price's *Kate Vaiden*, contemporaneous with Michael Dorris's *A Yellow Raft in Blue Water*, employs this same central temporary gap to similar effect. However, in contrast to Dorris's novel, Price's resolution of his temporary gap is not sufficiently consonant with his characterization of Kate (his abandoning mother), and is the point (its very end) at which this engaging novel elicits textually dissonant reader-resistance in conflict with its psychosocially mimetic genre.

Much of *Kate Vaiden* works to successfully authenticate its narrator and invite reader complicity. Kate has an orphan's fear of being abandoned. Her parents die in a murder-suicide when she is eleven; she first expresses her fear of abandonment to her aunt Caroline ("So I said 'Don't ever leave me'" [58]). She silences her aunt's attempt to discuss the possibility of her (Aunt Caroline's) death ("I rolled right to her and said 'No,' loud. I wouldn't have another person near me die" [74]).

Kate has an early sexual and emotional attachment to a boy a couple of years older than herself. Gaston Stegall, her young lover, is drafted at the end of high school; their last year together is shadowed by World War II and Gaston's approaching military service. But Kate, wrestling with her fear of being abandoned, tries denial:

> Sometimes alone I'd tell myself to brace for the day he'd be called up (they let you finish school). I'd walk around feeling pitiful and brave for an hour or so, but the fear wasn't real. Maybe in the four years since Dan and Frances [Kate's parents] died, I'd pulled a thick curtain on even the <u>idea</u> that people could swear they needed you one night, then vanish by morning. (102, original emphasis)

Gaston is drafted immediately after finishing high school and commits suicide at boot camp. This seems to convince Kate that love is so threatened by loss that she cannot risk it, and that there is something about her that perhaps causes the deaths of those she loves. After Gaston's death, her cousin Fob, meaning to comfort Kate and Gaston's father, tells them "It'll happen again" (125). Kate thinks "he wasn't wrong" and feels a recognition in that thought ("It somehow changed me" [126]). Kate hears in Fob's remark an affirmation of her fears, and Gaston's death instigates the solitary wandering that will become the pattern of her life. Kate decides, after losing so much love in Macon, that "the place itself was ruined" (124) and, with the freedom of money given her by Fob, she can go to her uncle Walter. Her fear of attachment becomes a conviction: "I thought of the night Caroline left me in the dark by Frances's Penny Show. <u>People would leave you.</u> I'd tried to forget that; time kept flinging me regular reminders" (144, original emphasis).

At Walter's home she meets another orphan—Douglas—who mirrors and clarifies her experience in some definitive ways. Kate sees it as "a secret awful as a poisoned well—orphans. . . . Not good enough magnets to hold even <u>parents</u>" (169, original emphasis). Douglas changes Kate's view of her experience from personal to universal; he gives her the name of orphan, which makes her experience appear to Kate (and to the novel's reader) as destiny. She calls her fear "<u>orphan</u> scared" (178, original emphasis) and begins the pattern of the next forty years: "<u>Leave people before they can plan to leave you</u>" (219, original emphasis). Douglas is a catalyst for Kate because he changes her perception of her history and her fate. Leaving Macon, Kate had felt she was freeing herself; her tragedies were linked to "the ground here, something you breathed"

(134). Douglas changes that perception, giving her the word "orphan" and the following story, a possible allegory for their lives.

> It was just a little story, called "The Growing Boy." A boy named Carl was put in an orphanage at five years old. Food was scarce and bad, and the rooms were cold. When they let him out at sixteen to make his own way, he ate everything that stood in his path or came too close. Nobody saw him do it; but things disappeared—doors on houses, privet hedges, a red-headed girl that tried to help him, the desk next to him at his place of work. He never got fat but he never got full, and nobody caught him till he died of old age with a big bank-account. The autopsy found all the stuff in him still, dead and shrunk but plain to see. (180–81)

Douglas writes this story while helping Kate with a homework assignment. "The Growing Boy" gives shape to Kate's other orphan-related conviction that she is responsible for the deaths of those she has loved (304, 314). These fears of being left and of causing death are seen by her older self, the narrator Kate, as having impelled her repeated leave-taking, and this view is given extensive textual support, inviting reader complicity. The actual separations are presented as generated by something almost mystical ("it was sweeping me off again—whatever thing seized me in corners and led me" [316–17]; "I felt like I'd felt more than one time before—an arrow shot from somebody else's bow, flinging away with no other aim than to go far, far" [199]). She feels herself "led on, planned for and protected" (247) now that Douglas has shown her that her experience has a source other than herself.

Narrator-Kate finds another source of character-Kate's behavior in her mother. "Only lately I've wondered if it isn't just Frances—my mother's blood in me, working for pleasure in the here and now (nobody under forty can believe how nearly everything's inherited)" (134, original emphasis). Introducing her story, she sees her mother as "the big question from my own early past. . . . Besides my son . . . the only human being I hope still to know" (9). Kate hopes to know whether her inheritance compelled her behavior. Just before she leaves Caroline and Holt for the first time, she puts on makeup and dresses in her new clothes for them. They are startled by her resemblance to her mother, and Kate worries that the resemblance might be more than physical. "Was there some part of Frances growing in me now—shining through my face—that would soon break out and hurt those harmless souls and God-knew-who-else?" (142–43).

"Who else" appears not long after: Kate has Douglas Lee's baby. She doesn't marry him, accepting that he cannot give her what she wants. ("I lay down again and listed a dozen things I wished he had said. The only one that could really have helped was some natural form of <u>Til death do us part</u>. What I've wanted all my life is the earnest sound of that from somebody" [200]). As long as the baby is still inside her, pregnant Kate feels confident that she has found "one thing that won't ever leave me" (212). Once the baby has separated from her body, that confidence is shaken. As a separate identity, Lee is another person with the power to leave her. And so she leaves her infant son, interpreting a baby's gesture as that familiar threat:

> But when I held a finger toward his hand, he didn't reach to take it. Then he looked away.
>   Even I wasn't fool enough to think he understood and had cast a No vote. Still, all these years later, I won't deny that I thought he'd turned away from me at a big crossroads. It left me with feelings that played some part in what I did.

Feeling that she would not be missed much, a feeling that accompanies her life and relationships (175, 201, 247, 347), Kate leaves her son with her Aunt Caroline and Uncle Holt, leaving as she first left Gaston at Annie Lee's home (107) and as she continues to do up to the point just before she feels herself change (357). This moment of change, appearing late in the novel's presentation of events, is the point where the older Kate, retrospectively narrating the story of her life, appears as a character. Kate ritualizes her break with her past by giving away a dogwood necklace (given her by Noony, Caroline's cook who had helped raise her) to a stranger who "had never said a civil word to me" (318). Narrating the events of her childhood and young adult life, Kate's voice is both vivid and authentic. The character-narrator's actions are thoroughly accounted for in her personal history and psychology, inspiring reader complicity. The novel has instructed its reader to append the explanatory "orphan" to the events of Kate's life. The orphan fears of being left and causing death, the orphan compulsive consumption allegorized by Douglas, the death of Gaston ("nobody

else, however strong and kind, quite promised me as much" [346]),
the similarity to Frances and the conviction that she was not
needed or missed much, firmly ground Kate's actions, persuasively
explaining the dramatic ruptures in her primary relationships.

Yet while the character's going away is well grounded in her characterization, her remaining away for decades is not. The narrator's
voice breaks in explaining why she stayed away for so many years.
Duration[2] is short—most of the novel is given to tales of young Kate,
with very little text allocated to most of the character's life. Kate
says that her "life stopped there" (317), that is, after her attempt
at integrating past and present by telling a lover about the child she
had abandoned. This attempt ends in his leaving her, and in her
acceptance of the impossibility of reconciling her past with her
present. She can only describe herself as having slept through
those years. "Thirty-five years passed. And if you don't imagine the
average human can sleep that long, let me swear I did . . . the real
Sleeping Beauty never dimmed out more completely than me"
(338). So inadequate is this explanation that she gives a contradictory one, saying also that she consciously adopted a way of life that
contained no close ties, emulating her former elementary school
teacher:

> I watched how she acted in all her circles, how much she gained and
> gave, how seldom she was hurt. In the years I watched her, one old
> friend died of a sudden stroke—no lingering sadness. So I thought I'd
> try to live like that.
>   And I did, more or less, through the years till now. (325–26)

Kate makes some dubious claims for the wisdom of her actions, describing herself as being "[with]out the mothering part . . . the tend-
ing rearing permanent patience and the willingness to take such
slim reward as most mothers get . . . [were] left out of my soul completely" (346–47). She complains (the only complaint in the entire
history) that "[f]athers can walk out on whole nests of children
every day of the year and never return, never send back a dime—
that's considered sad but natural. But an outlaw mother is the
black last nightmare any man can face"(346).

A thirty-five-year sleep, the fortunate sparing her child her mothering ("Lee Vaiden's been lucky not to grow next to me" [346]) is
an unconvincing resolution of the temporary gap of maternal ab-

sence in the text. Kate's claims that she had not hidden herself, that she could have been found had she been needed, and that she had followed the local newspapers fearfully throughout the Vietnam War (knowing her son was of age for military draft) are not consistent with the strength, honesty and thoughtfulness of her characterization and of the narrative voice of the story before this point. Because Reynolds Price is mimetically psychosocial (as he describes in an essay on the writing of *Kate Vaiden*), attempting to "write in a female voice" that would be "a credible expression of my mother's own spiritual potential" (Price 1989: 376–77), this thirty-five-year "sleep" is a gap the resolution of which is unacceptably inconsistent with the novel's narrative voice. (The identification of author and narrator on this point is an interesting one. Price's narrator Kate expresses her wish to know her dead mother, saying that "[b]esides my son . . . [she is] the only human being I hope still to know" [9]. Price affirms his search for his own dead mother's voice in the novel he narrates through Kate [1989: 376–77].) The act of cross-gendered storytelling is, for him, one that provides access to "total human sympathy" (1989: 375) and "new and usable modes of understanding . . . portable from the page into life" (1989: 376). It is this psychosocial emphasis of the novel and its sustained reader complicity that is disrupted late in the novel with Kate's brief explanation of decades of maternal absence, creating reader resistance in a narrative strategy that seeks (and for most of the novel achieves) reader complicity, undermining that essential primary relationship of the novel, author-reader.

On Permanent Gaps

Daniel Defoe's *Moll Flanders,* two-and-a-half centuries older than Reynold Price's *Kate Vaiden* and Michael Dorris's *A Yellow Raft in Blue Water,* offers an interesting analogue—and contrast. All three novels share the central gap of women abandoning their children without explanation, but in *Moll Flanders* the gap is permanent. Moll Flanders is strikingly inattentive to her children, but the social focus of Defoe's novel makes the permanence of the gaps in her narrative acceptable to the reader. She has and leaves several children, sometimes accounting for them and sometimes not. She expresses contradictory feelings, occasionally claiming great emotion and often callously departing. About her first two children, the children of her five-year marriage to Robin, she says they "were indeed taken happily off my hands by my husband's father and mother, and that was all they got" (52). The reasons for abandoning her children are economic. She cannot support them herself and/or find a husband to support her, burdened as she is by children. These reasons are consistent with the sturdy voice of the survivor who tells her tale with great charm, accepting life's upheavals (she describes her second husband as having "left me by the necessity of his circumstances" [108]). It is in describing her feelings for her children that the narrator is inconsistent. After describing her separation from her first two children indifferently (as their having been "happily taken off my hands") and vengefully (as "all" her inlaws got from her), fifty pages later she declares that "it was death to me to part" with a child, though she recognizes the necessity of separation as "the danger of being one time or other left with him to keep without being able to support him" (109). The child she is agonizing over here is her fifth, the survivor of three children she had by her Bath lover. So concerned was she initially that she wrote her lover for a settlement that would enable her "to be near him [the child] my self too, that I might have the satisfaction of seeing him, without the care of providing for him" (109). And yet, once she writes this letter, she considers herself "a single person again" (110), and we hear nothing more of this child, the arrangements made, or any attempt by his mother to see him.

Finding the thought of abortion "abhorrent" (140, 146), Moll has more children. As it was always an "inexpressible misfortune . . . to have a child upon my hands," she has to dispose of them in order to have a chance at remarrying, with marriage essential for her survival. The child she has with James is the only other child over whom Moll grieves at parting ("it touch'd my heart so forcibly . . . that I could not think of it without horror" [15]). She was aware that the child could be "murther'd, or starv'd by neglect and ill-usage" (150). Moll even moralizes on the point:

> to neglect them [children] is to murther them; again, to give them up to be manag'd by those people who have none of that needful affection plac'd by nature in them, is to neglect them in the highest degree; nay, in some it goes farther, and is in order to their being lost; so that 'tis an intentional murther, whether the child lives or dies. (151)

Feeling so strongly about the child she had with James, Moll "was upon the point of giving up my friend at the bank"; that is, choosing the child at the sacrifice of a prospect of marriage. Recovering herself, Moll makes arrangements to give up her child, with provision for visitation contingent upon additional payment (153–54). Although Moll makes a point of keeping up the payments for as long as she can (171), there is no indication that she actually exercises her visitation rights.

Moll has two children by her fifth and last husband (164), who dies when she is forty-eight years old. It is his death that begins her criminal history. Her initial response to his death is to cry for two years (165) for fear of poverty; she does not mention what her children did those two years. Then she describes the arrangements she made: "I enter'd into some measure to have my little son by my last husband taken off; and this [the caretaker] made easie too, reserving a payment only of 5.1 a year, if I could pay it" (172). Moll does not seem to remember that she had two children, not just one, by this last husband.

In America for a second time, Moll has her only reunion with a child, one of the three children she had with her brother (before discovering their sibling relationship [77]). At the time she left that husband, she "thought fit to tell him thus much, that he neither was my lawful husband, nor they lawful children, and that I had reason to regard neither of them more than I did" (82). Leaving for England, Moll shows great concern for establishing conditions for her own maintenance and makes no mention of thoughts of her children. Yet on seeing one of her American children again, before making herself known to him, Moll kisses the ground where he has passed and weeps (279). Meeting her son, she is speechless, overcome with emotion, tearful (289). Recovering, she promises him an inheritance, as she "had no child but him in the world" (292), forgetting those she had deposited in different parts of England. Moll is a charismatic character and a forceful narrator, but these are enormous gaps in the text, and they are never closed. Why then does the reader of *Moll Flanders* overlook these gaps? Why is reader complicity unaffected by them?

Ian Watt, an agile reader of *Moll Flanders*, suggests that

in reading Defoe we must posit a kind of limited liability for the narrative, accepting whatever is specifically stated, but drawing no inferences from omissions, however significant they may seem . . . our interpretation should not be allowed to go beyond what is positively stated by Defoe or Moll Flanders. (1957: 124)

Watt ascribes these gaps to "the desultory nature of personal relations in the criminal milieu" and finds a "laconic authenticity" (125) there. In other words, the social realism of the novel is what encourages the reader to overlook even major gaps such as these. In the contortions of reader complicity that the text shapes but that these gaps challenge, Watt conflates character, narrator, and author in accommodating them:

> Moll Flanders, of course, has many feminine traits. . . . But these are relatively external and minor matters, and the essence of her character and actions is, to one reader at least, essentially masculine. This is a personal impression, and would be difficult, if not impossible to establish . . .
> It is surely more reasonable to assume that all these contradictions are the consequence of a process to which first-person narration is peculiarly prone; that Defoe's identification with Moll Flanders was so complete that, despite a few feminine traits, he created a personality that was in essence his own. (126–28)

Watt is even seduced by Moll into claiming an anachronistic revolutionary status for *Moll Flanders* and its author, as he calls "Defoe . . . a welcome figure . . . because he seems long ago to have called the great bluff of the novel—its suggestion that personal relations are the be-all and end-all of life" (15).

Reader complicity in such "calling of the novel genre's bluff"—or at least in accepting a careless and casual abandonment of children—is encouraged both by the cross-gendered narrative mode of *Moll Flanders* and its exclusive focus on social (rather than psychological) realism, a narrowing of focus no longer possible in the novel of the twentieth century. This chapter demonstrates reading through the fissures of narrative mode and temporary and permanent gaps in relation to genre. These fissures point to the failing textual moment in Reynolds Price's *Kate Vaiden,* and contrasting success in Daniel Defoe's *Moll Flanders* and Michael Dorris's *A Yellow Raft in Blue Water*. The impact of these fissures on reader complicity and resistance also illuminates questions of narrative integrity whose ethical implications I discuss in this book's epilogue. But first, having read to the end of narrative I return to its beginning, to questions of writing narrative. Shifting focus to the more obviously generative half of the writer-reader collaboration that constitutes narrative, Part II discusses ways to apply and incorporate the skills of reading through textual fissures to writing a more reflectively reflexive metanarrative.

Part II
Rhetoric: Using Fissures—Writing the Metanarrative

Rhetoric: Using Fissures—
Writing the Metanarrative

THIS SECTION IS MORE TENTATIVE THAN THE FIRST AS IT ATTEMPTS TO
build on the critical reading skills surveyed in Part I and translate
them into reflectively reflexive writing. Self-reflexive writing must
somehow textually incorporate awareness of the inevitable symbolic violence of the active-passive relationship between the writer
and the written-about. Bourdieu defines symbolic violence as "a
gentle violence, imperceptible and invisible even to its victims, ex-
erted for the most part through the purely symbolic channels of
communication and cognition" (Bourdieu 2001: 1–2, 59–60; see
also Bourdieu 2000 [1977]: 192–97). This section suggests rhetorical remedy, to the extent that it is possible to rebalance narrative
hierarchies, through reflexive use of the various textual fissures exemplified in the readings of Part I. The aim of Part II is to begin to
conceptualize generically different metanarratives for all disciplines and professions that involve both reading the story and telling the tale of that reading. To that end, its focus is the
ethnographer's craft, on *reading* informant's narrative and *writing*
the ineluctably interpretive metanarrative.

Clifford Geertz has grappled with this problematic for forty years.
His early writing focuses more on reading tasks, while his more recent work, reflecting contemporary rhetorical concerns in many
fields, is concerned with "negotiating the passage from what one
has been through 'out there' to what one says 'back here'" (1988:
78). "Thick description" was an early articulation of the ethnographer's task of reading and writing culture(s). As he describes it in
his pioneering essay "Thick Description: Toward an Interpretive
Theory of Culture":

What the ethnographer is in fact faced with . . . is a multiplicity of complex conceptual structures, many of them superimposed upon or knot-
ted into one another . . . which he must contrive somehow first to grasp

85

and then to render. . . . Doing ethnography is like trying to read (in the sense of "construct a reading of") a manuscript. (1973: 10)

In Geertz's view, the ethnographer's work is analogous to that of the literary critic (1973: 9; 1988: 78). In his most recent book, viewing the ethnographer's field as comprised of "texts, or . . . 'text-analogues'" (2000: 17), his focus turns from "doing ethnography" to the challenge of writing responsively and respectfully about others:

> Comprehending that which is, in some manner or form, alien to us and likely to remain so, without either smoothing it over with vacant murmurs of common humanity, disarming it with to-each-his-own indifferentism, or dismissing it as charming, lovely even, but inconsequent, is a skill we have arduously to learn, and having learnt it, always very imperfectly, to work continuously to keep alive; it is not a connatural capacity, like depth perception or the sense of balance, upon which we can complacently rely. (2000: 87)

This study seeks to take its place in this process of learning and working. As we have seen in Part I, the tools of the literary critic are not confined to the fictive and have much to offer readers of narrative in all fields. In the matter of writing, however, literary studies are struggling with the same challenges as Geertz's ethnographer, and the inscriptions of this struggle are written across and through metanarratives, as a more responsive writing begins to emerge.

Viewing our own metanarratives in terms of Kenneth Burke's conception of symbolic action is helpful here in its insistence on the "necessarily *suasive* nature of even the most unemotional scientific nomenclatures" (1966: 45, original italics). Self-reflexive writing would then aim to expose its own rhetoric to its reader's scrutiny and to arouse its reader to active engagement with the text. The challenge is great, since both what we see and what we say are in some senses predetermined by the limitations of our own perspectives. As Burke puts it:

> Not only does the nature of our terms affect the nature of our observations, in the sense that the terms direct the *attention* to one field rather than to another. Also, *many of the "observations" are but implications of the particular terminology in terms of which the observations are made.* In brief, much that we take as observations about "reality" may

be but the spinning out of possibilities implicit in our particular choice of terms. (46, original italics)

I emphatically agree with Burke, excepting only the qualifiers ("many" and "much") to these statements. In my view, our observations and their articulation are always also—but not only—determined by our framing terms. We cannot step outside our own frame and achieve an Archimedean perspective[1]. This incapacity obviously limits the ability of the symbolic action of self-reflexive narrative to mitigate the inherent symbolic violence of writing. From the perspective of the written-about, this imbalance always inevitably remains. The channel of meliorative action is through the writer-reader relationship, which is the focus of this book.

Although we cannot find a perch outside ourselves from which to read and write of others, we continue to look for better rhetorical balance. Seyla Benhabib's conceptualization of "generalized" and "concrete" others offers a theoretical frame of "interactive universalism" that can be useful to writers. In her generous and somewhat fluid view of self-other exchange, Benhabib suggests and maps a more encompassing concept of alterity that embraces both shared and individual aspects of the other and "regards difference as a starting point for reflection and action" (1992: 153). She conceptualizes these shared and individual aspects as generalized and concrete others, a relationship dynamic but not agonistic. I quote her somewhat at length here, as I want to suggest application of this theory to the writing of metanarratives.

Benhabib describes the standpoint of the generalized other as requiring

> us to view each and every individual as a rational being entitled to the same rights and duties we would want to ascribe to ourselves. In assuming the standpoint, we abstract from the individuality and concrete identity of the other. We assume that the other, like ourselves, is a being who has concrete needs, desires and affects, but that what constitutes his or her moral dignity is not what differentiates us from each other, but rather what we, as speaking and acting rational agents, have in common. Our relation to the other is governed by the norms of *formal equality* and *reciprocity*: each is entitled to expect and assume from us what we can expect and assume from him or her. (158–59, original italics)

Note that she describes these perspectives as ones we "assume"—that is, adopt or put on—an important element of this theorization of otherness. In self-reflexive writing, a utilitarian awareness of perspective as assumed for a purpose—not inherent, not a given—is crucial.

This generalized other is one part of the interactive universalism envisioned by Benhabib. Partner to the generalized other is the concrete other, which requires

> us to view each and every rational being as an individual with a concrete history, identity and affective-emotional constitution. In assuming this standpoint, we abstract from what constitutes our commonality, and focus on individuality. We seek to comprehend the needs of the other, his or her motivations, what she searches for, and what s/he desires. Our relation to the other is governed by the norms of *equity* and *complementary reciprocity*: each is entitled to expect and to assume from the other forms of behavior through which the other feels recognized and confirmed as a concrete, individual being with specific needs, talents and capacities. Our differences in this case complement rather than exclude one another. (159)

This is both an epistemological issue and a political one, a question of knowing and acting, reading and writing. Contextualization is the methodology of concretization in both reading and writing. As readers, we must inform ourselves as thoroughly and profoundly as possible. As writers, we are obliged to particularize, including, of course, consideration and articulation of our own positioning and perspectives.[2]

Translating Benhabib's theory of interactive universalism into self-reflexive and other-inclusive rhetoric is the challenge of writing the metanarrative. It has been prompted by an increasingly self-aware public, an external pressure on writers to somehow undo (or at least expose) hierarchical and oppressive power structures in the professions and in the academy. The interaction between generalized and concretized otherness broadens and deepens our capacity to engage with each other, a great gain in the social sphere. But the rewards can also be personal. The process of concretizing otherness, with its need of contextualization and information, can be a significant part of the process of individuation that Jonathan Lear, reading psychoanalysis philosophically, posits as a lifelong human potential. Writers can play an important role in continuing to stimulate this potential, both in ourselves and in our readers. In this regard, it is instructive to listen to Lear's explanation for the life-long duration of the process of individuation, often misperceived as ending with the onset of adulthood. Lear writes that

> [p]sychic structure can continue to develop because the world outstrips my ability to appreciate it. As I develop in complexity, so does the world as it exists for me. The internalization of structure can thus continue at ever higher levels of complexity and refinement. . . . Since the development of psychic structure can continue throughout life, this task of individuation can be reenacted at ever higher levels of complexity. (1990: 177–78)

Facilitation of a continuing process of individuation (for ourselves and, at least in aspiration, for our readers) at varying and advancing levels of complexity offers an invigorating and self-renewing approach to writing. Benhabib's theorization of generalized and concretized alterity suggests a method.

Realizing that method rhetorically is the challenge that Part II surveys. In Part I, the more developed methodologies of reading generated by the fields of linguistics and narratology offered the possibility of looking at reading through separating (partially and for the sake of demonstrating) textual features as fissures offering hermeneutic entry. That is not yet available for discussion and characterization of reflectively reflexive writing. Self-reflexive writing is an emerging genre (as I call it in chapter 5) whose outlines are becoming increasingly visible. To sharpen that visibility, this section focuses on a single fissure, that of narrative mode, and its implications for writing metanarrative.

Part II is divided into two chapters intended as the nucleus of a conversation[3] on the rhetoric of ethnography. Chapter 5 examines rhetorical strategies of participant-observer ethnography; chapter 6, rhetorical strategies of ethnographic fiction with a shared topos of ritual human sacrifice. These two chapters are organized and analyzed through a two-tiered comparison: within chapters, linking texts as reciprocal figure and ground, reading the voices in the texts against that changing perspective; and between chapters, juxtaposing real-life and fictional ethnographies. Chapter 5 describes a genre of ethnography forming in response to participant-observer fieldwork in anthropology. Four contemporary works are analyzed in terms of their rhetorical strategies and stated aims. These voices are generic pioneers, self-consciously (with all the limitations that implies) creating a genre more responsible toward and more responsive to their informants—a genre foregrounding its narrative fissure as an ethical stand. Chapter 6 describes two ethnographic fictions that share a thematic focus of human sacrifice but differ interestingly in their choices of narrative mode. I return here to fictional narratives to explore available narrative modes and their implications. In this application and appropriation of fiction, I again follow Paul Ricoeur. Writing is a retrospective art, and "[i]t is precisely because of the elusive character of real life that we need the help of fiction to organize life retrospectively" (1992: 162). The extent of the reciprocity between fictional and real-life narrative is not my concern here. The borrowing and exchange are applicable as long as they are useful, and their utility will be decided—and, I hope, extended—by my readers. The juxtaposition of these chapters, the first reading ethnography and the second ethnographic fiction, illuminates aspects of writing by opening the fissure of narrative mode and analyzing its rhetorical power in these different but related narrative texts and contexts.

5

An Emergent Genre

A Woman Sings a Song for a Soldier Come Home

The wound kills that does not bleed.
It has no nurse nor kin to know
Nor kin to care.

And the man dies that does not fall.
He walks and dies.   Nothing survives
Except what was,

Under the white clouds piled and piled
Like gathered-up forgetfulness,
In sleeping air.

The clouds are over the village, the town,
To which the walker speaks
And tells of his wound,

Without a word to the people, unless
One person should come by chance,
This man or that,

So much a part of the place, so little
A person he knows, with whom he might
Talk of the weather—

And let it go, with nothing lost,
Just out of the village, at its edge,
In the quiet there.

—*Wallace Stevens*

THIS CHAPTER DISCUSSES ATTEMPTS OF LATE-TWENTIETH-CENTURY ethnography to "sing" suffering. Like the woman of the title of Wallace Stevens's poem of unspeakable suffering, like the poet for whom she is a metaphor, contemporary ethnographers approach and "sing" areas of human experience once limited to artistic communication. I consider here whether ethnography has a language sufficient to articulate and contain this topos. As Clifford Geertz has noted, for such scholarship, "[t]here seems to be a genre missing" (1995: 120). My focus is on the problematic of an emergent invented genre and its challenges, reflecting on ways that ethical problems in this field have created a respondent and correspondent poetics.

The contemporary ethnographer is often a participant observer, differently vulnerable from her predecessors (Behar 1996), though the struggle to position the personal in the professional is being experienced in all fields today. What shifts self-referentiality to self-reflexivity is the positioning of the speaking voice and its representation, an awareness and exposure of narrative point of view, "a point of view on a point of view" (Bourdieu 1996: 34). "Wittgenstein compares undisciplined thought to a fly trapped in a bottle. The philosopher shows it the way out. So do the economist and the psychologist. Literary texts tell us what it's like to be the trapped fly" (Bercovitch 1996: 251). This is also the move that ethnography has made, from outside to inside the bottle; in Benhabib's terms, toward greater concretization. Moving inside is also a strategy for avoiding "casting the social sciences in the image of the natural sciences, and [. . .] general schemes which explain too much" (Geertz 1995: 127). It is a strategy for "raising doubts [. . .] about all the preconstructions and all the presuppositions, both of the researchers and the respondent" (Bourdieu 1996:29), a dubiety that is reflected in both the methodologies of research and in its representations. Reflectively-reflexive writing aspires to such Bourdieusian skepticism in creating its implied reader, a critical reader anticipated and embodied in the text, a reader attentive to narrative fissures as entryways into the text.

The critical empathy of the participant observer (what Pierre Bourdieu calls "mentally putting herself in their place," "situat[ing] herself at the point in social space from which the respondent views that space," [22, 33]) is given written expression in the self-reflexive writing of this ethnographic genre. "[O]rdinary people's speech [is given] the same skilled attention elsewhere revealed in interpretative struggles to understand Shakespeare or the Bible" (Fowler, B. 1996: 14). The literary-critical skills of attending to texts, listening to textual voices and silences, determining the registers of speech and the point of view of the speaker are some of the elements of this essential "skilled attention" (and the focus of Part

I of this book). It is an ethnographer imagined in a literary critical (rather than a scientific) mode who can interpret the "hesitations, repetitions, sentences interrupted and prolonged by gestures, looks, sighs or exclamations, . . . laborious digressions, ambiguities . . . , references to concrete situations, [and] events" (Bourdieu 1996: 31), and tell their stories. I now proceed to look at the discursive styles that have thus far emerged from the representational struggles of participant-observer ethnography, narrowing the field to sharpen the focus by looking at ethnographies with a shared topos of suffering.

ETHNOGRAPHY AS LITERATURE

> The question for cultural studies is not to be or not to be, but
> _how_ to be, disciplinary. The answer, I think, is to use disciplin-
> arity against itself, and my proposal to that end is to see cultural
> "texts" in literary "context."—Bercovitch (1996: 248)

As ethnography struggles to create discursive styles to represent contemporary anthropological sites, it has moved generically closer to literature, consequently inviting anthropologists and ethnographers to acquire skills previously primarily employed in literary studies. The interdisciplinary nature of a thematic unity of focus (such as the current anthropological interest in suffering) creates what Arthur Kleinman calls the ethnography of experience, a genre that necessarily generates new strategies of seeing and telling. "[T]he materials required to understand suffering are of such a different order that we believe research approaches to it must deal directly with an experiential domain that heretofore . . . has been the grounds of art" (Kleinman 1995: 118). Pursuing this insight, this book suggests ways that the field of literary study can provide essential tools for this ethnography (and similar writing in and between other disciplines), since the study of literature is "more transparently _constructed_ than any other textually based body of knowledge, . . . [and] it highlights the constructedness of all disciplines" (Bercovitch 1996: 248).

Exposure to and training in literary studies, rhetorical analysis, narratology, critical discourse analysis, and related fields offer tools to study text and context with rigorous and systematic attention. The ability to create a textual work of art, disciplined by science and anthropology, while concomitantly remolding and rewriting them both, seems the most persuasive method to encompass and accommodate the challenges of representation taken up by ethnographic narratives of suffering. This emergent ethnographic genre attempts to capture something of "the perplexing multiplicity and inexpediency of experience" (Kleinman 1999: 74) through a narrative multiplicity which includes, but is not limited to, authorial perspectives. As Geertz asserts in his 1988 essay: "It is not clear just what . . . imaginative writing about real people in real places at real times exactly comes to beyond a clever coinage; but anthropology is going to have to find out if it is to continue as an intellectual force in contemporary culture" (141). It is this emerging genre that I proceed to examine in the discursive strategies of four contemporary ethnographers: Vincent Crapanzano in *Waiting: The Whites of South Africa* (1985); Renato Rosaldo in *Culture and Truth; the Remaking of Social Analysis* (1989); Ruth Behar in *The Vulnerable Observer: Anthropology that Breaks Your Heart* (1996); and Nancy Scheper-Hughes in *Death Without Weeping; The Violence of Everyday Life in Brazil* (1992) (with her later alternative ethnographic narrative, "Ire in Ireland" [2000]).

DISCURSIVE STRATEGIES OF THE EMERGING GENRE

Ethnography has increasingly evolved from positioning itself as an apparently transparent gaze to a now audible voice that not only acknowledges but often insists upon itself as a continuously felt authorial presence. This move has frequently been labeled "reflexive," and it is on the baggy nature of this reflexivity in contemporary ethnography that I focus here. Reflexive writing ranges from the reflective to the merely self-referential. Reflexivity as reflection enhances the intersubjectivity of the ethnographic relationship. Self-referentiality at best replaces the illusory transparency of early ethnographies with a subjectivity strikingly limited in its engagement of the other; at worst, it is solipsistic. The various strategies discussed below aim to maneuver this reflexive potential toward reflection and away from the simply self-referring speaking voice.

Reflexive ethnographic writing can perhaps be measured as a move away from Geertz's observation that "so much of it [ethnography] consists in incorrigible assertion" (1988: 5). This "incorrigible assertion" is common to both the guise of transparency of classical anthropology and the merely seemingly reflexive anthropology that is actually inordinately or primarily self-referential. Another way of distinguishing the self-reflective from the self-referential in reflexive ethnography is by an eyewitnessing that is not merely I-witnessing, but rather polyphonic testimony that reconceptualizes the Foucaultian author-function as shared (Foucault 1980). This maximally multivocal testimony may help to alleviate what Geertz describes as the heavier burden of authorship of contemporary ethnographic texts, resolving the clash he notes between "author-saturated texts and those of author-evacuated ones" in a shared authority textually represented (1988: 138). This matter of textual representation of intersubjective authority is essential. It is not enough to answer the methodological problems of fieldwork; as Geertz observes, "no matter how delicate a matter facing the other might be it is not the same sort of thing as facing the page" (1988: 10).

In addition to a move away from assertion and toward polyphony, reflexive ethnography makes new demands on its readers. Responding to "a sort of epistemological hypochondria" (Geertz 1988: 71), narrative polyphony demands greater hermeneutic participation by readers in texts not necessarily epistemologically unified. In Geertz's felicitous definition, this ethnography is

> a rendering of the actual, a vitality phrased, enabling conversation across societal lines—of ethnicity, religions, class, gender, language, race—that have grown progressively more nuanced, more immediate, and more irregular . . . in a world where, tumbled as [people] are into endless connection, it is increasingly difficult to get out of each other's way. (1988: 143, 147)

Arthur Kleinman extends the imperatives of reflexive ethnography to include a kind of ethnographic teleology, a "working out what to do in terms . . . potentially generalizable" rather than mere "ideological positioning" (1999: 80, 85). Kleinman's insistence on "not only comparison and evaluation but also action" (70) offers an ethical articulation particularly acute for the ethnography of suffering, a witnessing that aims "to be of use" (88) on two levels. Ethnographic utility is reflected both in a generative sense of instigating action and in an translocal sense of more generalized applicability.

Contemporary anthropologists both participate in and theorize about this emergent genre. Focusing on perpetrators of suffering and illustrating the mechanisms of dominance ensnaring both dominant and dominated, Vincent Crapanzano (1985) writes reflexively in a theoretically self-conscious mode, explicitly evoking Bakhtinian heteroglossia and dialogism.[1] In *Waiting*, his study of whites in South Africa, Crapanzano uses the direct speech of his dramatis personae together with his first-person framing narrative. These multiple first-person narratives are his solution to the complicated power relations of informant-ethnographer, while his articulation of this solution reveals how intractable this problem is. Crapanzano tells us that: "Insofar as possible, I have allowed the white South Africans with whom I lived and worked as an anthropologist to tell their own stories" (xiii). The dominance dilemma inherent in ethnographic writing is vividly conveyed by the verb "allowed," in contrast with the expressed desire that informants "tell their own stories." More subtly, he writes in a double-voiced first-person narration that expresses his dual positioning as fieldworker/witness and anthropological-theorist. It is the combination and amalgamation of these speaking voices that represents and enacts Crapanzano's belief in an inner freedom that is expressed by a kind of vitality of interpersonal engagement (20–21) in an exemplary integration of literary form and conceptual framework.

Stylistically, Crapanzano manipulates syntax and pronouns to emphasize complexities of positioning. He uses a plethora of "I"-led sentences that serve a dual purpose, a self-reflexivity that serves both as a signal to the reader of positioning and a caveat of limited perspective. Often these "I"-led sentences are repeated in a single paragraph, rhetorically opposed by "They"-led sentences later in the same paragraph. Take, for example, these sentences excerpted from a single paragraph:

> I did not come to South Africa as a neutral observer. I came morally and politically outraged at the brute, unmediated legislation of human inferiority. I was filled with horror. . . . I had an almost mythic image of the perpetrators of this inhumanity. I was horrified by the depths to which humans will sink to preserve their trivial privilege . . . I indulged myself in my horror and disgust and learned later that my indulgence was itself a symptom of the "system." I met many white South Africans who were equally horrified and disgusted. Paradoxically, their horror

and disgust rendered their life in South Africa tolerable. . . . Tales of banning, detention and imprisonment, torture . . . were common. **They** appeared daily—as scandals in the English-language press, with caution in the Black and Coloured press, and with moralistic pretension in the Afrikaans press. **They** were talked up, especially in the cities where in "liberal" circles they produced a sort of hysterical heat. **They** were loudly denied in conservative circles, or somehow justified. . . . **They** were a sort of living folklore. (23, my emphasis)

These pronouns eloquently map the survival strategies of apartheid South Africa, while also positioning the speaker within the reality he is describing. The distancing maneuvers of the different population strands are united, as suffering is represented through and as "tales," banished by all (English, Black, Colored, Afrikaans) to the third person. In other words, the narrative strategy here insists on the reader's attention to this commonality, in spite of the different communities' responses (ranging from hysteria to denial to justification). The narrative thus demonstrates—through its use of pronouns and of syntactical repetition—how it is that people accommodate terrible suffering that they cannot help being aware of. The varying tone of the responses is secondary to their shared essential distance. Furthermore, as the speaking voice moves from the condemnatory safety and ideological clarity of its I-view, the paragraph enacts the inevitable corruption of all participants in a corrupt society, subverting the possibility of distance between his "I" as he sees his initial stance reflected in those of his informants.

This first-person and third-person opposition presented with syntactical repetition makes implicit second-person demands (on the reader), insisting thereby on the partiality of the narrative report and thus on the hermeneutic responsibilities of the engaged reader. These demands and responsibilities are particularly acute in the study of a racist society where language use inevitably implicates the speaker. As Crapanzano notes:

Each time I use one of the racist terms—"white," "Coloured," "Asian," or "Black"—or refer to "Afrikaners" or "English," I am participating in a particular self-interested constitution of social reality, which I find morally reprehensible and which does not, in any event, do justice to the human reality it purports to describe. I am forced to think that reality, and I am not alone. It is thought by the whites of whatever persuasion and by the peoples of color as well. (28; see also 35)

Crapanzano's consequent heightened sensitivity to language use is richly applicable to all social study, a primary tool in exposing textual ideologies.

After alerting his reader to assume a critical stance even to his own narrative, Crapanzano similarly structures his metanarrative, letting his informants speak in their own voices. Thus, for example, Hennie, one of Crapanzano's informants, enacts the dual blindness and insight that Crapanzano insistently reminds us is a feature of all perception. Attesting to his struggle with the Dutch Reformed Church of his Afrikaaner background (which he ultimately abandoned in favor of his "English" wife's Anglicanism), Hennie describes the struggle for control reflected in the tension between figurative and literal interpretations of the biblical texts so essential to Afrikaaner self-definition and identity. His church forced him "to accept the fact that the world and everything in it was made in six days, . . . [not allowing for] an idea of gradual evolution, even though there was plenty of evidence around me for it" (94). Yet, as his first-person testimony often reveals, Hennie himself is frequently limited in his ability to apply what he has learned about the relationship between language, dogma and "evidence around [him]." Stylistically, Crapanzano is using the problematic reliability of the first-person narrator to highlight (and not resolve)[2] epistemological questions for his reader. In this multivoiced metanarrative, Crapanzano demonstrates the quality theorized by Willis and Trondman as exemplary ethnography—"the showing of relations of indeterminacy embedded within the social," a representation expressive of "a critical and dialogical consciousness" (2000: 9)—and breaks significant stylistic ground in creating a reflectively reflexive genre of ethnography.

The relationship between fieldworker, informant, and reader is cast somewhat differently in Renato Rosaldo's seminal work in the genre, *Culture and Truth* (1989). Rosaldo's triangle echoes that of Shakespeare's Lear-Gloucester-audience, a generous synaesthetic exchange where Gloucester's "seeing feelingly" leads to Lear's offer: "If thou wilt weep my fortunes, take my eyes" (4.6.178). Viewing thought and feeling as a constitutive whole (106–107) and professional imperative (173), Rosaldo describes how his personal experience of the rage in grief changed and enhanced his understanding both of his fieldwork and of his writing. His experience of rage in his grief over his wife's accidental death illuminated for him the practice of headhunting among the Ilongots (perpetrators of suffering within the framework of this discussion) that had previously been unfathomable. As both fieldworker and ethnographer, he reconceptualizes "the positioned (and repositioned) subject," "prepared to know certain things and not others" (7–8). Rosaldo describes an epistemological obstacle overcome through a central life experience, his subjectivity enhancing his intersubjective understanding. Signaled by an initial "Thus" (8), Rosaldo describes this process of personal and professional interrelated insight. Extending this relationship to his reader, Rosaldo explains his "use of personal experience . . . as a vehicle for making the quality and intensity of the rage in Ilongot grief more readily accessible to readers" (11), who "should be as informed as possible about what the observer was in a position to know and not to know" (69, and see also 184). Mary Louise Pratt, a literary scholar looking cross-disciplinarily at ethnography, maps this move somewhat more formally:

> Personal narrative mediates this contradiction between the engagement called for in fieldwork and the self-effacement called for in formal ethnographic description, or at least mitigates some of its anguish, by inserting into the ethnographic text the authority of the personal experience out of which the ethnography is made. (1986: 33)

Rosaldo's theorizing on ethnography is founded on an understanding that "no mode of composition is a neutral medium" (49). Extending Bakhtinian intertextual heteroglossia to anthropology as a discipline, he envisions a kind of cross-disciplinary intertextual polyphony consisting of "diverse legitimate rhetorical forms [which] will allow for any particular text to be read against other possible versions," enabling anthropology "to approximate people's lives from a number of angles of vision" (62) that "cannot necessarily be added together into a unified summation" (93). This polyphonic intertextuality would include the "distanced normalized description" of classical anthropology (with its "ethnographic present") but would deny its exclusivity (184), emphasizing the need for narrative multiplicity in cultural representation. Rosaldo thus offers us not only a view of an emergent genre but also of the changed discipline that this implies, one that includes "narrative as a form of knowledge" (130). This expanded anthropological epistemology necessitates an ethnographic toolbox similarly expanded to encompass narrative analysis through textual fissures such as those I have been demonstrating. The methodological anchors of critical discourse analysis, focusing on representation and rhetoric where "there is not necessarily any true reality that can be unveiled by critical practice" (Fowler, R., 1996: 4), offer textual anchoring to the qualitative researcher. Thus trained, the social analyst can better achieve Rosaldo's ideal of imaginative positional exchange enhanced by professional collaboration (189).

In *The Vulnerable Observer* (1996), Ruth Behar walks through the door opened by Rosaldo and expands the opening. Daring to push the limits of the genre, Behar inevitably pushes against them in an interesting example of this ethnography, a self-consciously reflexive text that offers a close look at both the resources and the risks of the genre. In a single paragraph of the introductory essay that gives its title to her book, Behar exposes the poles of the reflexive potential enacted in her book—reflection and solipsism. Recognizing that the ethnographer's personal narrative "is only interesting if one is able to draw deeper connections between one's personal experience and the subject under study," Behar asserts a prerequisite "keen understanding of what aspects of the self are the most important filters through which one perceives the world and, more particularly, the topic being studied" (13). Self-reflexive literature has the capacity for greater engagement with "the subject under study" through this kind of keen awareness and involvement. Yet this insightful articulation of the necessary frame for reflexivity is preceded in that same paragraph by the complaint that "[i]t is far from easy to think up interesting ways to locate oneself in one's own text." Mere self-referential writing and its inherent limits are well defined by this imaginative self-location.

   These authorial actions—distinguishing significant and connecting filters as opposed to imaginatively imposing one's textual presence—can help us distinguish between the self-reflective and the self-referential in reflexive ethnography. The distinction which Behar makes between "essential to the argument" and "decorative flourish" (14) is one she occasionally loses, creating an apparent polyphony of a many-in-me, citing "the ethnographer in me," the "feminist in me," the "novelist in me" (20), rather than a plurivocal many and me (which includes but is not limited to the multiple identities comprising that "me"). This seeming polyphony leads toward self-referentiality. The slippage from self-reflexivity to self-referentiality is not a problem of pace (as Behar worries on page 18) or thematic focus (84). Its source is in the originating impulse of this writing, defined by Behar as "a desire to embed a diary of my life within the accounts of the lives of others that I was being required to produce as an anthropologist" (19).

The potential generic vulnerability of this ethnography, exposed in the theoretical section of her book, is also manifest in its ethnographic sections. Looking at nature and finding in it living metaphors for her grief at the death of her grandfather, Behar incidentally offers us a metaphor for the seductive breaking point of I-witnessing. Describing her final days of fieldwork on "death and memory" in northern Spain, she tells of a melancholy walk in the countryside on an unseasonably cold and windy July day, "looking for mirrors of my sorrow" (1988: 71). This tendentious mirroring, expressed earlier as the impetus for her writing, leads the reflexive away from reflectivity and closer to referentiality. Behar evokes Kafka's metaphor for successful writing ("A book must be an ice-axe to break the sea frozen inside us") in a scaled-down version of her own ("at least an ice pick" [86]). The ice-pick metaphor is illuminating in its retention of classical ethnography's power relations, expressed in this objectification of the reader as one whose responsiveness must be released by the agency of the ice-pick-wielding author. It is this slippage between self-reference and reflectivity that may account for what Behar experienced as "the surprisingly ruthless criticism of the humanists" (164) in response to her work, and which maps for us at least the parameters of this complex emergent reflexive ethnography.

The work of Nancy Scheper-Hughes (who, like Behar, looks reflexively at victims and suffering) offers additional insights into the forging of a challenging and critically engaged social science. Her book *Death Without Weeping* offers "an anthropology-with-one's feet-on-the-ground" (1992: 4). In interesting contrast to Behar's "anthropology that breaks your heart," Scheper-Hughes's anthropologist is *both* vulnerable *and* politically engaged. Reflecting and refracting the postmodern reluctance to evoke colonialist interventions, her writing raises therein core issues in the ethics of ethnography. Her fieldwork, and most directly, her informants, demanded an exchange of goods, insisting that they would oblige the "antropologa" that she had become only if she would resume work as the "companheira" she had been years earlier when working at the same site as a Peace Corps volunteer (15–18). In responding to the demands of her informants for advocacy and constituency, Scheper-Hughes attempts to evolve a professional perch that continually confronts, though doesn't pretend to resolve, "vexing questions of moral and ethical relativism," offering "the beginnings of a moral and an ethical reflection on cultural practices that takes into account but does not privilege our own cultural presuppositions" (21–22).

For Scheper-Hughes, ethical responsiveness is characterized by "compassion toward the others" accompanied by "[a]ccountability, answerability to 'the other'" (1992: 22–23). Always inherently partial, ethnographic understanding emerges out of a hermeneutic imperative <u>shared</u> by ethnographer-informant-reader but <u>belonging</u> to none. Conceived by Scheper-Hughes as "the working out of an ethical orientation to the other-than-oneself," this ethnography is born of an anthropology that seeks to ameliorate suffering (1992: 26) while refraining from colonizing sufferers, "an ethical and a radical project . . . transformative of the self but not (and here is the rub) transformative of the other" (1992: 24). This parenthetically voiced awareness of the central difficulty in realizing this professional ideal is underscored by the single nonnegotiable element of the anthropological work described by Scheper-Hughes: "[W]hat may never be compromised are our personal accountability and answerability to the other" (1992: 24). Professional responsibility includes both telling tales and keeping counsel in textual silences (salient fissures) mapped and emphasized by Scheper-Hughes, inviting interpretation without "blowing the cover" of her informants (1992: 508). On this point, Scheper-Hughes interestingly interrogates her earlier professional self, suggesting that "the time-honored practice of bestowing anonymity on 'our' communities and informants fools few and protects no one" while promoting an illusory and dangerous authorial license (2000: 128).

Using the personal to make and enhance the "connections" that are both the subtitle of her prologue and the motif of her prose is Scheper-Hughes's discursive strategy in her 1992 study, rhetorically emphasizing what James Clifford calls "the message of partiality" (1986: 8). She creates a metaphor of ethnographer as artist (1992: xi–xii) and tells (almost as epiphany) of a childhood neighbor, an artist whose paintings defamiliarized the home site, show-ing "what *we* never thought to see" (1992: xi, original italics). Bakhtinian dialogism suggests a narrative model for Scheper-Hughes as it does for Crapanzano, along with consequently en-gaged and implicated readers who participate in a reading act which "make[s] them party to the act of witnessing"—vulnerable observers creating correspondingly vulnerable readers (Scheper-Hughes 1992: 25, xii, 30).

Yet Scheper-Hughes's work has been criticized for stumbling precisely at this point of authorial privileging. In her recent re-sponse to criticism of her study of familial and communal dynamics in rural Ireland of the mid-1970s, Scheper-Hughes offers an alter-native ethnographic narrative to the one she initially published (2000: 129–32). After an evasive prefatory attribution of the hostile local reception of her book to difficulties "any writer" (12) on Irish subjectivity would experience, she tells the story as she "might have said" it, conceding that she "may have misread important aspects of social life" (129). Recognizing the problematic of authorial selec-tion, she attempts to recover other perspectives in the story retold, framing them by "while I told the anecdote about . . . , I failed to tell the anecdote about . . ." (131) in the revised account.

Juxtaposing narratives, the strategy Scheper-Hughes belatedly adopts in rewriting her Irish narrative, is one that Crapanzano uses successfully in *Waiting* (published fifteen years earlier; see above). Yet there is a salient stylistic difference between "Ire in Ireland" and *Waiting* that makes Crapanzano's metanarrative far more im-portant generically. His narrative strategy was framed by subver-sion of his own authorial authority, an initial gesture that situates his narrative as one of several in egalitarian insight and blindness. Scheper-Hughes's revised narrative (a revision responding to infor-mants' hostility to her metanarrative) does not follow Crapanzano in pursuing self-reflexivity to fuller narrative expression. Her narra-tive persona retains and maintains full control of all discourse, telling and interpreting the stories of others. The revised metanar-rative repeats these activities with somewhat different contents and acknowledges possible mistakes. Yet Scheper-Hughes stops her at-tempt to write alternatively at the threshold of authorial power. As we can see in comparison with Crapanzano's earlier deconstruc-tion of authorial power, Scheper-Hughes's ethnography is essentially conservative, its revised inclusiveness sustaining traditional ethnographic hierarchies.

The informant-ethnographer-reader triangle must be one of vital exchange, "always agitated by permanent criticism" (Foucault, quoted in McKerrow 1999: 446). Arthur Kleinman, in his discussion of Scheper-Hughes, points to another possible feature of the emergent genre, moving from mimesis to real-life action. For Kleinman, the ethical imperative of the ethnographer is in the "effort at working out what to do in terms . . . potentially generalizable, . . . out of which will emerge an agenda for practical action" (1999: 80, 92). In Ruth Behar's extended metaphor, responding to readers' responses to her ethnographic persona, "when readers take the voyage through anthropology's tunnel it is themselves they must be able to see in the observer who is serving as their guide" (1996: 16). Taking up Hamlet's dying charge to Horatio, the contemporary ethnological imperative at the topos of suffering is to "draw thy breath in pain,/To tell my story," recognizing Hamlet's story in Horatio's and thereby in our own, singing thus (to return to my opening metaphor) *for* another.

6
Speaking the Unspeakable

> Literature clearly plays a significant role in orchestrating the language that validates or invalidates certain experiences as suffering.
>
> —Morris (1997: 40)

IF ETHNOGRAPHERS ARE STORYTELLERS, AS I SUGGEST IN CHAPTER 5, then ethnographic fiction is a rhetorically related field that can enrich our thinking about ways of writing metanarratives. This chapter looks at the narrative strategies of two ethnographic short fictions with a shared topos, ritual human sacrifice. D. H. Lawrence's "The Woman Who Rode Away" (1928)[1] and Charlotte Mew's "A White Night" (1903) offer interestingly different looks at what Edgar Allan Poe called "unquestionably, the most poetical topic in the world," "the death . . . of a beautiful woman" (Poe 1956 [1845]). Applying Seyla Benhabib's terms, Lawrence conceives of his protagonist as a generalized other; Mew's is far more concretized. This chapter will look through fissures of narrative mode, textual voices, characterization, register, and repetition to observe the processes of generalization and of concretization, and their effects.

The stories differ in their choice of narrative mode, Lawrence's a third-person (male-authored) story and Mew's a first-person cross-gendered (female-authored) story. Both plots center on the ritual sacrifice of a woman, and comparison demonstrates how their narrative strategies shape readers' stance toward the crime. Illustrating Richard Ohmann's assertion that "[l]iterary mimesis implicates the reader in an imagined society by making him party to the acts that imply it" (1973: 102), the narrative strategies of each of these similarly focused stories direct the reader to quite different attitudes toward their female victims. In "The Woman Who Rode Away," Lawrence sweeps his reader into his text along with the fic-

105

tional masses who witness the ritual sacrifice, encouraging reader complicity in the murder by sanctioning the act with the objectivity and distance associated with omniscient narration and through the intimacy and access offered by focalization through the protagonist. (Focalization is "the angle of vision through which the story is filtered in the text," "verbalized by the narrator though not necessarily his" [Rimmon-Kenan 1989: 43, 71].) In "A White Night," Mew uses her male witness-narrator to tell the story while concomitantly pointing to the impossibility of expressing the horror of the deed in words, thus emphasizing its horror and rousing reader resistance to the ritual sacrifice enacted.

GENERALIZED ALTERITY AND READER COMPLICITY

In "The Woman Who Rode Away," a woman's sacrifice is witnessed by a celebratory crowd and a complicit reader. The story, set in a remote area of modern Mexico, uses a third-person narrator to tell of the ritual slaughter of a white woman at the hands of the Chilchuis (the "descendants of Montezuma and the old Aztec or Totanic kings" [1928: 759]). Lawrence's story of ritual sacrifice is told in terms similar to the description of corresponding rituals by the Aztecs of ancient Mexico in James Frazer's ethnographic opus, *The Golden Bough*, published six years earlier. Lawrence deviates from Frazer's narrative, however, in one striking point: the sacrificial object. In Frazer's description of ancient Aztecian ritual, the victim was a male prisoner of war, "carefully chosen from among the captives on the ground of his personal beauty" (1922: 588). Lawrence's victim is "the woman who rode away," a change not only of gender but of status, the captive male of Frazer's narrative changed into Lawrence's willingly submissive female.

Both Frazer's ethnographic narrative and Lawrence's literary one use the third-person narrator of factual reportage[2] as they describe the months of ritual preceding the slaughter and the murder itself, with similar effect on the reader. Frazer's description of the sixteenth-century Aztecian festival of Toxcat and Lawrence's of its imaginary contemporary Mexican Indian equivalent both read the murder as inevitable, with detailed descriptions of the chain of ritual events leading to it given from the distance of third-person narration (with Lawrence occasionally focalizing through his victim, his narrator verbalizing an imagined access to her point of view). Similarly distancing, the protagonists of both narratives are never individualized; Frazer's victim is called "the young man" and Lawrence's simply "the woman." Both the ethnographic narrative (Frazer's) and the ethnographic fiction (Lawrence's) present their protagonist as a generalized other;[3] this lack of specificity contributes to the distancing effect created by both narratives.

In his treatment of the victim-protagonist, Lawrence's narrative differs interestingly from Frazer's. Frazer gives no description of the victim beyond the fact of his physical beauty and his status as prisoner-of-war. We know nothing of his prewar existence or his motive for joining the war that ended in his captivity and death. In contrast, Lawrence's characterization of the victim emphasizes her willing submission, thereby blocking reader empathy. This absolutism leaves no indeterminate elements to activate the reader into imaginative participation in her plight.[4] "The Woman Who Rode Away" rode away from an environment repeatedly described as "dead." Before her capture, she lives in "lifeless isolation" near a "thrice-dead little Spanish town" with its "sun-dried dead church, the dead portals, the hopeless covered market place, where, the first time she went, she saw a dead dog lying . . . stretched out as if for ever," a place inhabited by "[d]eadness within deadness" (756). Neither her husband nor her children mitigate that deadness for her—only a "peculiar vague enthusiasm for unknown Indians found a full echo in the woman's heart" (759). Thus after presenting the woman's life-in-death, preparing the reader to view her capture as a rescue, Lawrence continues his blame-the-victim characterization, describing her as "overcome by a foolish romanticism more unreal than a girl's. She felt it was her destiny to wander into the secret haunts of these timeless, mysterious, marvellous Indians of the mountains." (759). The woman's subsequent submission to captivity, humiliation, and death is thus grounded both in the imagery of the setting of her precapture life and in the "foolish romanticism" of her nature. She sets off on her journey toward death without "even turn[ing] to wave" good-bye to her servant or to her son, her implied maternal failings attesting to her deformed spirit.

Her journey takes her past the refuse of white male exploitation, "another deserted mining-settlement," "the now-abandoned mine," "another silent, long-abandoned mine." The imagery of her solitary journey echoes across the external images of desolation, as the woman is described as "feeling like a woman who has died and passed beyond. She was not sure that she had not heard, during the night, a great crash at the centre of herself, which was the crash of her own death" (761–62). This portrait of the woman as already dead is complemented by her change of feeling just before she meets the Indians. The elation of the first part of her journey has faded and "she began to go vague and disheartened." However, meeting the Indians seems to raise her spirits, becoming a rescue of sorts, as the narrator describes her "faint sub-smile of assurance," her "half-childish, half-arrogant confidence in her own female power" (763) as she "smiled faintly in the pride of her own adventure and the assurance of her own womanhood, and the spell of the madness that was on her" (764).

The woman is also portrayed as racist and a "spoilt white woman" (764), viewing the Indians as "just natives" and looking at their "long black hair with a certain distaste" (763). The narrator, exhibiting a different attitude toward the Indians, describes that same hair as a "river," "full of life," and "unrestrained." This meeting of white woman and Indian negates first her gender (the Indians "saw no woman at all") and then her life. Eight times in this short narrative she is described as "aware that she had died," her feelings presented as ranging from a passive acceptance of her fate to a thrilling to it: "The woman was powerless. And along with her supreme anger there came a slight thrill of exultation. She knew she was dead" (765). The victim's feelings, presented this way with the objectivity and authority of the third-person narrator and the imagined access to her point of view attained by focalization through the protagonist-victim, shape the attitude of the reader. The woman has been described as indifferent to family ties, totally self-absorbed, vaguely racist, and exulting (slightly) (765) at the prospect of her imminent death. As a result of this portrayal, the reader feels very little for the woman and her fate; indeed, the reader cannot feel more for the fate of this character than she herself does. Empathy is blocked.

The direct speech of the characters supports the narrator's characterization of the woman and provides no ground for reader empathy. It is her hubris that brings her to declarations such as "I came away from the white man's God myself. I came to look for the God of the Chilchui." Her detachment from herself and embracement of her fate are reflected in her speaking of herself in the third person.

> "Does the white woman seek the gods of the Chilchui because she is weary of her own God?" came the question.
> "Yes, she does. She is tired of the white man's God," she replied, thinking that was what they wanted her to say. She would like to serve the gods of the Chilchui. (769)

Presented as dead already and thus less than human, her inattention to the differences between literal and figurative language contributes to her participation in her own death. Through his translator, she is asked by the chief

> ". . . do you bring your heart to the god of the Chilchui?" translated the young Indian.
> "Tell him yes," she said, automatically. (771)

And, of course, it is literally the victim's heart, cut from the living breast, that is the object of the sacrifice that ends both Frazer and Lawrence's narratives.

The rituals leading up to the sacrifice are similarly described in both narratives. Both victims are given flowers, new clothing, feathers, and special housing. But while Frazer—basing his account on those written by the sixteenth-century Spaniards who conquered the Aztecs and wrote about their rituals—describes his victim as heavily guarded, Lawrence continually emphasizes his victim's willing participation. Frazer's account tells of eight guards whose captain would die in place of the prisoner if the captive escaped. Lawrence's narrative describes the woman as "will-less and victim to her own indifference" (776), and sometimes as even mystically enjoying her (mistaken) perception of her own power. With the assistance of a "sweetened herb drink," the "confidence in her own female power" (763) and "assurance of her own womanhood" (764) that the woman exhibited on first encountering the Indians turns during her captivity into

> a sort of heightened, mystic acuteness and a feeling as if she were diffusing out deliciously into the harmony of things. This at length became the only state of consciousness she really recognized: this exquisite sense of bleeding out into the higher beauty and harmony of things. . . .

She herself would call to the arrested snow to fall from the upper air. She would call to the unseen moon to cease to be angry, to make peace again with the unseen sun like a woman who ceases to be angry in her house. (779–80)

In other words, the woman has adopted the Indians' narrative as her own and has accepted her role in its resolution. The Indian myth, told the woman by her attendant, is that "The Indian got weak, and lost his power with the sun, so the white men stole the sun. . . . The moon, she is angry in a white woman's cave" (779). According to this myth, this usurpation of native by white will only be redressed "when a white woman sacrifice[s] herself to our gods" (778). The woman's acceptance is explained by the narrator thus: "The Indians, with their heavily religious natures, had made her succumb to their vision" (781). Her voluntary participation is presented as an essential element of the sacrifice, as the dialogues between the woman and the Indians continue to work the tension between literal and figurative language. When she first arrives in the village, she tells the chief: "I came away from the white man's God myself" (769). Later, when his son tells her: "We have lost our power over the sun, and we are trying to get him back," she answers: "I hope you will get him back." The insistent repetition of Lawrence's text has the attendant ask her to repeat an affirmation of her willing participation.

"Do you hope it?" he said.
"I do," she answered fatally.

This voluntary victimization in Lawrence's text is in marked contrast to Frazer's historical account of the presacrifice period, which emphasizes precautions taken against a possible escape and the coercion of the captive (588). In addition, the extensive use of force dominates the description of the moment of sacrifice itself in the historical narrative, when the Aztecian victim "was seized and held down by the priests on his back upon a block of stone, while one of them cut open his breast, thrust his hand into the wound, and wrenching his heart out held it up in sacrifice to the sun" (Frazer 1980 [1922]: 589).

In contrast, Lawrence's victim is never "seized." Rather, she is described without agency and without resistance, suggesting her continued collaboration: "And at length she was on the platform of the cave" (786). She is stripped on that platform, above and in front of "a strange amphitheatre" (786), to the cheers of the "throng below" (787). The Aztecian sacrifice, in contrast, was attended only by priests and took place at "a small and lonely temple by the wayside" (Frazer, 589). Lawrence's crowd cheers as the woman is presented to it frontally (as the narrator emphasizes "her strange pallor"), then turned so that "her long blond hair" can elicit a second cry from the crowd below. The woman's consciousness is reported in a manner implying a link with nature in the sacrifice she is about to make ("She knew that this was the shortest day of the year, and the last day of her life" [787]), and her emotions are reported as disengaged ("She felt little sensation, though she knew all that was happening" [787]). The reader, given the access to the character's mind and feelings that omniscient narration provides, is thus blocked from participating imaginatively and empathetically with the protagonist. The omniscient narrator, associated by the reader with the author, is what makes this story a reenactment, the reading a participation in the ritual, with "good continuation" (Iser 1978: 186) sweeping the complicit reader to its lethal conclusion. Just as the Indians "had made . . . [the woman] succumb to their vision," Lawrence makes his reader succumb to his. And what is Lawrence's vision of this story?

Lawrence tells the reader his vision in the tale's final line, emphasized through placement in a separate paragraph. The rationale of the sacrifice is the rationale of the story, an assertion of "[t]he mastery that man must hold, and that passes from race to race" (788). And, one might add, from man to man, the vehicle of mastery being woman. The alliteration and assonance of that final sentence are part of the overall pattern of word and sound repetition in the story, which powerfully propels the reader to its conclusion. This aural sweep of the reader is similar to the way the woman-victim watches "spell-bound, and as if drugged . . . all the terrible persistence of the drumming and the primeval, rushing deep singing, and the endless stamping of the dance of fox-tailed men, the tread of heavy, bird-erect women" (777). With the poetry of his prose Lawrence seals his text, ensuring "good continuation" and reader complicity as he attacks "[t]he sharpness and the quivering nervous consciousness of the highly-bred white woman." His stated aim—in the voice of his omniscient narrator—is to "obliterate . . . [h]er kind of womanhood, intensely personal and individual" in order to obtain a "womanhood . . . cast . . . into the great stream of impersonal sex and impersonal passion" (777). The authority of the omniscient mode of narration and the intimacy and access of focalization through the protagonist, together with its poetic prose, focused on Poe's "most poetical topic in the world," seduce the reader into complicity with the lethal exchange enacted in "The Woman Who Rode Away."

CONCRETIZED ALTERITY AND READER RESISTANCE

In "A White Night," Charlotte Mew picks up this same "most poetical topic in the world" to tell quite a different story. Her self-reflexive story immediately raises problems of mimetic fiction and points to its narrative mode with a layered narrative structure. The introductory narrative is composed of two paragraphs. The first is given in direct speech by Cameron, the male first-person narrator of the main narrative; the second is a one-sentence paragraph by the authorizing narrator, first-person but ungendered. The authorizing narrator claims accuracy for the transcription of Cameron's narrative, recorded "the night he told it . . . almost word for word," the narrator promising the reader that "you have the story as I heard it" (146). Cameron's direct speech in the introductory narrative begins the story with the declaration that "[t]he incident . . . is spoiled inevitably in the telling." He despairs of adequately telling "things as they are," while asserting the possibility of telling things as they *were*, claiming that accuracy improves with historical distance: "Make it a medieval matter—put it back some centuries—and the affair takes on its proper tone immediately" (146). In this oddly confident claim for the accuracy of historical over literary narrative, Mew's character (who two paragraphs later becomes her narrator) speaks in a voice distinctly different from the author of this multivoiced text, as this reading will show.

In his direct speech in the introductory narrative, Cameron begins to shape the reader's attitude to his subsequent narrative and Mew begins to create the resisting reader implied in her text. Cameron complains that, in the telling, "[t]he subtlety, or call it the significance, is missed, and unavoidably, as one attempts to put the thing before you, in a certain casual crudity, and inessential violence of fact" (146). He laments that "a recollection, an experience, a picture . . . doesn't reproduce; one must have the original if one is going to hang it on one's wall," a desire that becomes grotesque when we discover, six pages later with the first scream of the woman victim, that this is a tale of human sacrifice.

Setting and characterization are part of the concretization that shapes reader response in this story. Mew sets her main narrative specifically as to time and place (in Spain, spring 1876). The human sacrifice at the heart of this story is witnessed by three characters, the narrator Cameron, his sister Ella and her husband King. Ella and King are on their honeymoon, having come to Madrid from Florence; Cameron is getting ready to leave Spain after spending eighteen months there "on mining business." The concreteness of Mew's text is part of its insistent realism, in contrast to the generalness of Lawrence's narrative that is part of its strategy of achieving mythic significance. In the same way and to the same ends, Mew's quotidian language of life contrasts with Lawrence's elevated register of myth.

The three set out to explore "those wilder districts which at best, perhaps, are hardly woman's ground" (146). This characterization by Cameron of the country through which they were traveling at the time of the events that he recounts exemplifies the Bakhtinian dialogism, the double-voiced discourse, of this story. Cameron means, of course, that travel through that part of the country was difficult, without amenities, as he goes on to describe his sister as traveling easily while her husband "on occasion nursed anxiety . . . and mourned his little luxuries" (146). As the reader encounters what Cameron calls "the eventual, central scene" (147), the ritual sacrifice of "one of the loveliest" (152) of women, we realize that this is "hardly woman's ground" in a far more menacing sense.[5]

In the six pages that Mew gives Cameron to "[t]ell the details of that day," the day preceding the deadly night of the title during which the three travelers witness the ritual sacrifice, the act of bearing witness is emphasized and thematized. Concomitantly, the point of view of the narrator begins to be questioned as his reliability (that gesture of distancing of author from narrator) is subtly undermined. Many elements of this early distancing of author from narrator are seen only retrospectively on a first reading, just as the grotesqueness of Cameron's desire to "have the original," expressed in the introductory narrative, cannot be seen as such until halfway through a first reading when the "central scene" of human sacrifice is revealed.

In his description of their travels, Cameron begins by praising his sister's skillful handling of their "human instruments," a puzzling phrase that is clarified in his next sentence where he declares that Ella "took our mule-drivers in hand with some success" (146). Describing the remote town in which they set up camp and from which they set out that day, Cameron says that it "made a claim to something like supremacy of charm. There was the quality of diffidence belonging to unrecognized abandoned personalities in that appeal. . . . [A] city with a claim, which, as it happened, I was not to weigh" (147–48).

This begins the characterization of the narrator as an amoral figure, one who fails "to weigh" even such a weighty act as the murder he witnesses, as we see by his direct speech in the introductory narrative and later on in his own narrative. His subsequent descriptions of the female victim of the sacrifice and his response to her are reflected in what he describes as the source of the charm of the town, the "diffidence belonging to unrecognized abandoned personalities" (147). Read in light of the murder revealed later in the narrative, which is anticipated here as "the eventual, central scene," this description of the town characterizes its speaker as appallingly deficient in moral sensibility, as we begin to hear the author's voice through his narration and as we hear confirmed at the end of the story by Ella, the only female witness to the murder.

The three travelers set out from the town toward evening, passing an inn whose mark of habitation is an open door through which they hear some swearing, and a church, which seems uninhabited though not a ruin. The church is described as "impressive in its loneliness, its blank negation of the outside world, its stark expressionless detachment, . . . resolutely lifeless" (149). The narrator finds that "this absence of a human note was just," describing the scene in what Roger Fowler calls generic sentences, a style that "claims universal validity for a general assertion" (Fowler: 1981, 112). Generic sentences subtly mask their point of view and their ideology within the present or past simple tenses of factual description. The narrator then changes to a more blatant universalization of his point of view, using an agent but keeping it the third-person neuter "one," claiming that "[o]ne didn't want its solitude or silence touched, its really fine impersonality destroyed"—asserting thus general public status for the personal view of the speaker. This "really fine impersonality" that the narrator claims "one didn't want . . . touched" is echoed in his description of the "impassive company" of monks, whose indifference to their screaming victim is then repeated in Ella's accusation of insensibility to the narrator at the end of the story. As Mew creates her resisting reader through limiting the reliability of her narrator, she extends that resistance here to universalization as a speech act. Cameron conflates the "one" of the universal with himself, giving his opinion the false authority of the universal. Mew highlights this assumption of universality by having her narrator shift from his initial generalizations in the form of generic sentences to the more transparent universalization of masking personal opinion by the seemingly neutral third-person "one." The effect of these language shifts within the fissure of universalization is to alert the reader to pay closer and more skeptical attention to the narrator's speech acts.

The human sacrifice that the three travelers observe takes place in the middle of the night in the privacy of the seemingly abandoned church, with about fifty monks attending and no audience. Lawrence's takes place in daylight and in public, displayed to a crowd of people. In these very different settings we can also see something of the authors' attitudes toward Poe's "most poetical topic in the world." The repeated emphasis on darkness in Mew's story colors both the deed itself and the witnessing, both the attitude of the text toward its "central scene" and toward its narrator. The horrible deed can thus only be told by a narrator of limited vision, literally in terms of his position as witness in a darkness cut only by the monks' tapers and morally in terms of his failure to "weigh" the significance of the event. This failure is pointed out to him by his sister Ella at the end of the story, yet its persistence is shown in the moral blindness of his subsequent narration (in the represented time of the fabula, the narrative viewed chronologically), given at the beginning of Mew's story. Viewing events retrospectively, the narrator describes events in aesthetic terms as problems of narration in mimetic fiction and an appreciation of the theatricality of life. In other words, the aestheticism of the narrator is displayed by the author to reveal the horror of the ideology behind Poe's "most poetical topic in the world."

The procession of monks chants as it enters the church, a chant by "unmistakably . . . men's voices" that the narrator describes as "a music neither of the sense, nor the spirit, but the mind, as set, as stately, almost as inanimate as the dark aisles through which it echoed; even, colourless and cold" (151). This "music of the mind" is pierced by the screams of the woman victim as the witnesses hide themselves "behind one of the pillars of the apse." The narrator qualifies his description of the monks by a parenthetical "(about—and at a venture)," guessing as to their number. Through this concretization, these details—the precision with which Mew positions her narrator behind a column and the hesitation with which he qualifies an unimportant detail—Mew reminds her reader of the limited <u>moral</u> vision of her narrator as he begins to unfold what he has described as the "central scene." Describing the monks who continue their procession oblivious to the cries of the woman, he tells us that "on the whole impassive company her presence, her disturbance, made no mark. For them, in fact, she wasn't there" (152).

For the narrator, the woman is there as part of a theatrical event. While his description of the monks' indifference to their victim asserts the narrator's very different view of himself, Mew's fissure of universalization shows the reader their similarity. In the universalization of generic sentences, Cameron states his view that "[s]he wasn't altogether real, she didn't altogether live." He introduces the qualification "at least as I was viewing it" only to modify his subsequent claim that the woman's presence gave the scene "its only element of life," reverting to the universal "one" to make his claim for the victim's participation in the narrator's theatrical metaphor for her murder. "She had, one understood, her part to play; she wasn't, for the moment, quite prepared; she played it later with superb effect." The resisting reader that Mew shaped earlier in her text is alert to and takes a skeptical stance toward the narrator's universalizations. The narrator's extended metaphor of theater dominates his description of the murder. The victim's face is described as "a mask, one of the loveliest that spirit ever wore" (152). The narrator frees himself by this metaphor of having to identify with the victim's humanity, asserting that her "mask . . . gave no clue" as to her feelings. The author, however, indicates her presence through duration (a "temporal/spatial relationship," the relation between the duration of the event in represented time and the length of text given it [Rimmon-Kenan 1983:52]). She spends two paragraphs speculating on the victim's feelings in the form of the narrator's questions about "it," her mask and its present and past emotions. The dialogism of this part of Mew's text is thus in the tension between the language of the narrator, particularly in its imagery, and the organization of time in relation to text by the author. In this way, Mew displays the horror of the aestheticism of objectifying woman, letting her male narrator speak the convention so succinctly given by Poe while she reminds the reader of the subjectivity of the object and the moral blindness of the aestheticism of this convention.

The narration of the ritual murder continues in the two forms of universalization (generic sentences and the neuter and seemingly neutral and objective third-person "one") that the author has alerted her reader to resist. When the monks stop their chanting, the narrator tells us, "one realized the presence of these men, who, up to now, had scarcely taken shape as actualities, been more than an accompaniment—a drone" (153). This substitution of "one" for "I" is an ideological move making the personal universal, one the author has displayed to her reader before the account of this "central scene." The narrator's description of his impression of the progression of the men in almost cinematic terms, while given in generic sentences, reminds us of his limited point of view: "They shifted from a mass of voices to a row of pallid faces. . . . There they were, spread out for sorting." As he watches, the murderers are objectified ("it") and aestheticized (as a frame for their victim's face). This panning of the scene continues:

> And then one lost the sense of their [the monks'] diversity in their resemblance; the similarity persisted and persisted till the row of faces seemed to merge into one face—the face of nothing human—of a system, of a rule. It framed the woman's and one felt the force of it: she wasn't in the hands of men. (153)

In this extreme setting of ritual murder, Mew obliquely but powerfully reminds her reader of what happens to men and women in patriarchy. Adopting Heidi Hartmann's definition of patriarchy "as a set of social relations between men, which have a material base, and which, though hierarchical, establish or create interdependence and solidarity among men that enable them to dominate women" (Hartmann 1981: 14), we can read this scene as describing the cost of living within that system. For men, it is the loss of aspects of individual identity; for women, it has far more lethal consequences. In patriarchy, men are "united in their shared relationship of dominance over their women; they are dependent on each other to maintain their domination" (Hartmann, 14). It is this mutual male dependence that is the motive of homosocial exchange, a virulent form of which is mythologized in D. H. Lawrence's "The Woman Who Rode Away," and whose exposure determines the narrative strategy of Charlotte Mew's "A White Night." Mew's display of the misogyny of male aestheticism such as Poe's is striking in the theatre metaphor that her narrator extends as the murderous moment approaches. The prayers of the monks are described as "satire," the ritual murder as "the performance" (154). In a blame-the-victim strategy similar to the one Lawrence uses, Mew's narrator excuses his own failure to attempt to rescue the victim (in contrast to his brother-in-law's attempt, which he prevents [156]). The narrator explains that "[p]ossibly I had caught the trick of her quiescence, acquiescence, and I went no further than she went; I waited—waited with her, as it were, to see it through" (154). Cameron, transported by his own metaphor of theatre, "experienced a vague, almost resentful sense of interruption, incongruity, when King broke in to ask me what was up." King's interruption reminds Cameron of his sister's presence—and the possible danger to her life—which he expresses as "the consciousness that this, so far as the spectators were concerned, was not a woman's comedy" (154). Through her narrator's creation of this odd genre, "a woman's comedy," the author points to his complicity and blocks that of her implied reader. In contrast, it is precisely this complicity of the narrator with the deed that Lawrence hides as he creates the complicit reader implied in his story.

Cameron silences his brother-in-law by reminding him of the danger to their lives, and quickly "turned again to what was going forward." The victim's clothing had been changed by the monks, described by the narrator as a good "change of setting," making "the mask . . . lovelier now and more complete." Her earlier "shadow of a smile" is seen in terms of a theatrical performance as a "slip," unlike the current "inspired touch" of her detachment "from all the living actors in the solemn farce" (154). He describes the next couple of hours of ritual preceding the murder in aesthetic terms, "[t]he grave deliberation of its detail heightened its effect" (155). The opening of the tomb in which the woman is buried alive is described by the narrator in terms of the plot of a story. It is an "impossible *denoument*" [original emphasis], which he accepts, the author speaking dialogically through the narrator in this diction of narrative, her self-reflexive story always pointing to its telling.

Cameron's aestheticism reaches ridiculously romantic heights as he views the final scene: "For to my view it was these men who held her in death's grip who didn't live, and she alone who was absorbently alive." This romanticism colors his view of his failure to come to her rescue. He again blames the victim:

> She stood compliantly and absolutely still. If she had swayed, or given any hint of wavering, of an appeal to God or man, I must have answered it magnetically. It was she who had the key to what I might have done but didn't do. Make what you will of it—we were inexplicably *en rapport* . . .
>   . . . I was backing her; it hadn't once occurred to me, without her sanction, to step in, to intervene; that I had anything to do with it beyond my recognition of her—of her part, her claim to play it as she pleased. (156)

Of course, the woman could have no clue that there was an audience to her sacrificial murder; as far as she knew, only participants were present. Mew's reader cannot, therefore, share her narrator's interpretation of events.

The narrator's interpretation of the victim's behavior as willing participant in a theatrical performance is further subverted by the author as she contrasts his behavior with that of the other characters. The narrator tells us that "King was in the act of springing forward; he had got out his revolver; meant, if possible to shoot her before closing with the rest." Conceding that such action "was the right and only workable idea," the narrator tells us that he persuaded King not to intervene with "the first deterrent that occurred to me, reminding him of Ella" even while admitting that "it was not for her [Ella] at all that I was consciously concerned. I was impelled to stand aside, to force him, too, to stand aside and see it through" (156). In the passive voice of this sentence, his failure even after the act, in narrative retrospection, to weigh the moral consequences of his action (and inaction) or to attribute agency to himself, the narrator is contrasted with his brother-in-law. Only after the ritual sacrifice is over can Cameron respond to King; only then can he see "what King had all along been looking at, the sheer, un-picturesque barbarity" (157). The living entombment is viewed by the narrator as the "final act . . . the supreme illusion of the whole." Attentive spectator, he realizes as the priests withdraw that he "was missing something" (157), then explains that it was the audio fea-ture, the men chanting and the woman screaming, that had stopped. Yet his narration reveals an awareness that he was missing something much more profound—"the human and inhuman ele-ments in the remarkable affair, which hitherto had missed my mind"—while the personification of "human and inhuman ele-ments" exposes the persistence of his failure to take responsibility for his active spectatorship. In his view, he doesn't miss something to do with humanity; rather, something missed him. It is at this point that his sister reenters his consciousness (and the narrative), the author reminding the reader of the female witness to the ritual murder. Ella is silent, "unstrung," and perhaps "she partially lost consciousness" as the men attempt a belated and futile rescue of the victim. Ella again disappears from the narrative as the three wait for morning and make their escape.

Ella reappears in the inn, making "no comment" but insisting on reporting what the narrator calls "the night's occurrences" to the British Consul. Silent until now, he describes her as "persistent to perversity" on this point. The consul reacts with an aestheticism similar to that of the narrator. Using free (unmarked) indirect speech, the author adds the consul's voice to her narrator's as the consul picks up the narrator's metaphor of theater: "He heard the story and was suitably impressed. It was a truly horrible experi-ence—remarkably dramatic—yes. He added it—we saw him doing it—to his collection of strange tales" (158).

The consul's refusal to act is presented in terms similar to the narrator's. The consul tells his guests that "[t]he country was . . . extremely rich in tragic anecdote." Echoing Cameron's perception during the murder, through King's reminder of Ella's presence, that "this, so far as the spectators were concerned, was not a wom-an's comedy," the consul (conflated with the narrator in free indi-rect speech) explains that "[t]he laws of Spain were theoretically admirable, but practically, well—the best that could be said of them was that they had their comic side."

Thus Ella confronts the difficulty of speaking about this "most poetical topic in the world"—her difficulty reflecting that of the author. Mew gives her sole female witness two sentences of direct speech in the final section of her story. The narrator persists in his strategy of universalization, asserting that his sister "refuses to admit that, after all, what one is pleased to call reality is merely the intensity of one's illusion" (159). His sister's response is blunt: "'Oh, for you,' she says, and with a touch of bitterness, 'it was a spectacle. The woman didn't really count.'" Conceding that, the narrator claims "more than that: it was an acquiescence in a rather splendid crime." He admits that "at the moment in my mind, the woman didn't really count," but insists on the victim's sanction. "She saw herself she didn't. That's precisely what made me see." What explanation does the narrator give for this view? He claims her murder an "honor" that satisfied "some pride of spirit or of race," and her cognizance of that honor the motivation for the victim's complicity in her own murder. This is a perspective rejected by Ella, who "hasn't ever understood, or quite forgiven me my attitude of temporary detachment." It is also a perspective rejected by Mew and the resisting reader she creates in her story.

Through the heteroglossia of her text, Mew illuminates the horror of the aestheticism of male objectification of the female as part of the homosocial exchange necessary to maintain patriarchy. Through the dialogism of the narrative voice speaking his point of view in words that resonate with additional meaning, through pointing insistently to the limited reliability of her narrator and to his strategy of universalization, through the consul's voice, heard in the free indirect speech of Cameron's narrative, and through the direct speech of her sole female witness, Mew weaves a circuitous challenge to Poe's deadly aestheticism.[6]

Rene Girard's study of sacrifice (1972) offers an interesting gloss on the sacrificial exchange enacted by Lawrence and challenged by Mew in these two stories. According to Girard, "society is seeking to deflect upon a relatively indifferent victim, a 'sacrificeable' victim, the violence that would otherwise be vented on its own members, the people it most desires to protect" (4). In order for sacrifice to achieve its purpose of "restor[ing] harmony to the community [in order to] reinforce the social fabric" (8), the scapegoat figure must resemble what Girard describes as "the *human* categories excluded from the ranks of 'sacrificeable'" (12) while remaining sufficiently other to prevent the possibility of retaliation. In the terms of this discussion, Girard is showing us the scapegoat potential of Benhabib's generalized other. Sacrifice, according to Girard, "is primarily an act of violence without risk of vengeance" (12). It has disappeared, he says, in societies where the judicial system, a form of public vengeance, has assumed its function of preventing societies from being overtaken by endless cycles of revenge. In my reading of these early-twentieth-century British narratives, I have shown how sacrifice persists as an element of private vengeance, visible in art, facilitated always by generalized alterity. Woman in many societies often exemplifies the contradictory attributes that Girard describes as belonging to the *pharmakos* of ancient Greece, a person maintained by the state until needed for sacrificial purposes, both "an object of scorn" and "surrounded by a quasi-religious aura of veneration . . . a sort of cult object" (95). This duality is reflected in the process of "making sacred" (the origin of the word "sacrifice") that is the sacrificial ritual, through which society achieves a "metamorphosis of reciprocal violence [dangerous because it has no end] into restraining violence [positive in that it is an end] through the agency of unanimity" (96). The unanimity that Girard notes as a requisite of ritual sacrifice is asserted by D. H. Lawrence in his choice of narrative mode, and subverted by Charlotte Mew in hers. Mew calls attention to the violence that unanimity, omniscience, universality, generalization, and aestheticism can conceal. As Girard shows in his analysis of the history of sacrifice, "the various 'scapegoat' phenomena are not the reflection of some ill-articulated guilt complex, but rather the very basis of cultural unification, the source of all rituals and religion" (302). Pairing these texts as reciprocal figure and ground and using that changing perspective to read the voices in these texts opens the fissure of narrative mode and exposes the violence of aestheticizing the objectification of women and of generalizing alterity. The ethical implications of narrative mode, glimpsed through the fissures in these two narratives of human sacrifice, are the final focus of this book.

Epilogue: Reading and Rhetoric—
Ethical Implications

Eᴛʜɪᴄᴀʟ ɪᴍᴘʟɪᴄᴀᴛɪᴏɴꜱ ᴏꜰ ɴᴀʀʀᴀᴛɪᴠᴇ ᴄʜᴏɪᴄᴇꜱ ᴀʀᴇ ᴛʜᴇ ꜱᴜʙᴛᴇxᴛ ᴏꜰ
the preceding section, Part II's discussion of writing the metanarrative. Part II suggests concrete and generalized otherness as a way
of conceptualizing the writing subject and promoting a rhetorical
reflexivity that keeps the two in dynamic interaction. This final section, framed as an epilogue as it extends that ethical subtext and
brings it to the center of attention, focuses on a single key fissure—narrative resolution. Bernhard Schlink's *The Reader* and the
two (differently concluded) versions of Ariel Dorfman's *Death and
the Maiden* provide the field for a consideration of endings and
their implications. Highlighting the fissure of resolution in this, the
concluding section of my own metanarrative, is of course also a reflexive gesture, the final moment of my mimetically structured narrative that aims both to analyze and to enact reflective-reflexivity in
reading and writing narratives.

   The fictional field of this section looks at narrative as a "socially
symbolic act" (Jameson 1981)[1] in three realistic fictions of different genres (novel, play, film) with a shared topos of posttraumatic
personal and social recovery. Schlink's novel is set in post-Holo-
caust Germany, and Dorfman's play and film in "the present . . . ;
the place a country that is probably Chile but could be any country
that has given itself a democratic government just after a long period of dictatorship" (1994: 1). These settings sharpen the focus of
this epilogue on resolution and closure in narrative, as this formal
feature is also thematically central to these narratives of the often
conflicting claims of truth and reconciliation in newly democratic
societies. In Dorfman's words, his plot had to take place

> not in a nation under the boot of a dictator, but in one that was in tran-
> sition to democracy, where so many Chileans were grappling with the
> hidden traumas of what had been done to them while other Chileans
> wondered if their crimes would not be revealed. (1994: 48)

Following Paul Ricoeur, the readings in this book also seek to "examine in what way narrative, which is never ethically neutral, proves to be the first *laboratory of moral judgment*" (1992: 140, original italics). Authorial choices of narrative resolution are key experiments in that laboratory.

Political fiction of recent history (history within the memory or reflecting the contemporary circumstances of its readers) is ethical fiction with a job to do in the world—to provoke, instigate, appease, reconcile. Thus the threshold of resolution, the final moment of reader suspension within and without the narrative, is a moment of great significance. The desire for a closure unattainable in life can be realized fictionally. Indeed, closure of some sort must be achieved, since novels, plays, and films do end, leaving their reader to meet another day. Ricoeur's laboratory metaphor illuminates the way in which the liminal moment of narrative resolution leads back to life.

Briefly, the argument here is that the overly resolved endings of Schlink's novel and Dorfman's film function to let the reader/audience off the ethical hook salient to both (in ways according with other choices throughout both narratives), and that Dorfman's play does not.[2] One measure of ethics seen through the fissure of narrative resolution is thus an integrity within the narrative between questions asked and answers given.

Bernhard Schlink's *The Reader* (1997) tells the story of its narrator's adolescent affair with a woman more than twenty years his senior, and his accidental reencounter with her years later, when he was a law student observing a trial of women who had worked as concentration camp guards. This woman, Hanna, thus changes from a protagonist in the narrator's personal narrative to an allegorical figure in a nation's attempt to carry its murderous past, and the narrator himself changes into a double for his generation of Germans, children of both perpetrators and acquiescent citizenry. This change takes place in the very center of the novel, and from that point on the novel repeatedly points its reader to this allegorical reflection on the hard choices of Germany's second generation. The older narrator, looking retrospectively at his younger self (the law student unexpectedly encountering his personal and political pasts in a courtroom) articulates the central dilemma of his generation thus:

What should our second generation have done, what should it do with the knowledge of the horrors of the extermination of the Jews? We should not believe we can comprehend the incomprehensible, we may not compare the incomparable, we may not inquire because to inquire is to make the horrors an object of discussion, even if the horrors themselves are not questioned, instead of accepting them as something in the face of which we can only fall silent in revulsion, shame, and guilt? To what purpose? It was not that I had lost my eagerness to explore and cast light on things which had filled the seminar, once the trial got under way. But that some few would be convicted and punished while we of the second generation were silenced by revulsion, shame, and guilt—was that all there was to it now? (104)

The plural "we of the second generation" that identifies the narrator with his peers is also a self-reflexive move linking author to narrator.

From its beginning, Schlink's narrative leads to the release of its overly resolved ending. Characters are given reasons or circumstances extenuating their choices. Michael Berg (the narrator) is only a teenager when he is initiated by and becomes sexually enthralled to Hanna, age and passion combining to limit his accountability. This limited accountability is shared by the reader as a consequence of narrative mode: point of view is limited to that of the narrator's younger self, with the reader knowing no more than the narrator at any given moment. Limited accountability is later extended to Hanna. We learn that the central propellant of her life and its choices was a need to hide her illiteracy, a need that led her to take a job as a concentration camp guard rather than accept a promotion that would have revealed her problem. The most serious charge against Hanna is that in the course of the death march that she helped supervise, her charges burned to death as an Allied bombing raid hit the church where they had been locked in for the night. The five women guards, resting outside the church, could have released the several hundred women prisoners and saved them. They did not, and only two women survived the fire. The women guards subsequently submitted a report that falsified that history. At the trial, the other guards claimed that Hanna had written the report, a charge that Hanna, still committed to keeping the secret of her illiteracy, does not contest.

While the narrator says that Hanna's illiteracy and the pride that drove her to hide it are not extenuating circumstances, Schlink's

narrative enacts that extenuation in two ways. First, the novel miti-
gates the horror of Hanna's criminal choices by reducing its dimen-
sions to a logical chain of events stemming from a single
identifiable cause, her illiteracy. In addition, the narrator (and here
the author-narrator identification of "we of the second generation"
is relevant) characterizes Hanna in ways that complement that
view. She

> wanted to do the right thing. When she thought she was being done an
> injustice, she contradicted it, and when something was rightly claimed
> or alleged, she acknowledged it. She contradicted vigorously and admit-
> ted willingly, as though her admissions gave her the right to her contra-
> dictions or as though, along with her contradictions, she took on a
> responsibility to admit what she could not deny. . . . She had no sense
> of context, of the rules of the game, of the formulas by which her state-
> ments and those of the others were toted up into guilt and innocence,
> conviction and acquittal. (109–10)

The second mitigating move is Hanna's question and its answer,
given in direct speech. In response to questioning about selections
of prisoners for work or death camps, the other important charge
against her, Hanna asks the judge "so what would you have done?"
(111). The judge deflects her question from himself by a vague answer framed in the third person: "There are matters one simply
cannot get drawn into, that one must distance oneself from, if the
price is not life and limb" (112). The implication here is that the
person sitting in judgment of Hanna has far less integrity than
she does, as she is portrayed as something of a noble savage, igno-
rant of the ways of the world and its victim. This image is later extended in the characterization of the prisoner Hanna, who, having
learned to read, reads (of course) about the Holocaust.

This brief description of some of the ways the novel's two main
characters are released from full responsibility for their actions indicates the ways the novel ultimately does the same for the society
it portrays, and for its reader. The narrator asserts this link repeatedly ("the pain I went through because of my love for Hanna was,
in a way, the fate of my generation, a German fate" [171]) in a
claim for the larger significance of this politically realistic fiction.
Through the encounter between young Michael and Hanna, a generation older, and through the narrator's self-positioning as "we of

the second generation," the narrative thematizes that generation confronting its past. It is at this point that *The Reader*'s greatest evasion is staged.

Hanna serves her prison term, and Michael reads entire books onto tape for her, sending these tapes to her at the prison but never visiting her. When she writes him a note of thanks, he understands that she has used her time in prison to learn to read and even to write. Michael continues to send tapes but not to write, eventually receiving a note from the prison warden about the pending release of Hanna, granted clemency after having served eighteen years of her sentence. As Michael is her only correspondent, the warden asks him to visit and to attend to preparations for Hanna's release. He does so, and Michael and the reader are presented with the issue at the heart of this novel: How does the second generation live in relation to its seniors, "those who had committed Nazi crimes or watched them happen or looked away while they were happening or tolerated the criminals among them after 1945 or even accepted them" (169)? This is a confrontation he had dreaded earlier and had been spared by the judge's refusal to re-lease Hanna on her own recognizance during her trial. Then he'd understood that if she were released, "I would have to prepared myself to meet her again, and I would have to work out how I wanted to do that, and how it should be" (98). With her release, that meeting outside courtroom and prison, postponed earlier, has finally come.

Here Schlink rescues his narrator (and thereby his narrative) from this encounter by having Hanna commit suicide on the morn-ing of her release. Thus Schlink frees his narrator from facing the ostensible focus of the novel, the generation-after German working through his Nazi heritage. This, the novel's apparent thrust, is in reality its core failure. The narrative teleology has led to an evasion greater than that of Hanna's judge. The judge was asked about an imaginary past, the third conditional "what would you have done." The novel asks, and then evades, a present dilemma of what to do. If, as I am suggesting, an integrity between questions asked and an-swers given is one measure of ethics in narrative, Schlink's facile ending illustrates an ethical failure.

Ariel Dorfman's *Death and the Maiden* offers a fascinating compari-son and contrast to Schlink's novel viewed through the fissure of narrative resolution. Dorfman wrote his play (1991) one way and the film script of that play (1994) another. *Death and the Maiden* tells the story of three characters: a woman victim of torture and rape during a military dictatorship, her then boyfriend now husband (a lawyer just appointed head of a presidential commission investigating "human rights violations that ended in death or the presumption of death"), and a stranger who may or may not be the rapist. The audience is presented with two narratives—that of Paulina, the victim, and that of Roberto, the doctor perhaps-perpetrator—about crimes that took place some fifteen years earlier. Rape usually has no witnesses, and Dorfman's play enhances potential doubt by adding the blindfolding of the victim to questions of memory over time. Paulina identifies the stranger as her rapist first by his voice, later by his smell and by the touch of his skin. She surprises him, assaults and binds him, and Gerardo, Paulina's jurist husband and the man she saved by not giving any information under torture, is the judge she appoints at the trial she stages in their home.

The play and film are resolved somewhat differently, and that difference is crucial to audience response. The play, Dorfman's initial version, implicates its audience in the problem of living with—and acting within—uncertainty. The audience is left bearing the burden of the questions the play raises through the decision not to offer a clear resolution unshadowed by doubt. Dr. Roberto Miranda may be the doctor who supervised torture and who raped Paulina, but Gerardo (and his double, the audience) cannot be sure. Gerardo's persistent fantasies of closure reflect those of most of us, even in situations that he has described as "beyond repair" (5). He asserts a belief in the power of the publication of his commission's official report to "establish objectively" what happened and to ensure that "our country will never again live through" similar atrocities (6). In his marriage, he believes that it is possible "to start all over again" (26) and free themselves of the past, to "close this book once and for all" (36). For Paulina, closure is possible for human-scale failures such as Gerardo's replacing her in his bed two months after her disappearance, while she was undergoing torture and protecting his identity (37). But for the violations of torture and rape, closure is not possible. Roberto confesses and then denies his confession, claiming that he'd used information supplied by Gerardo to forge a realistic confession and save his life. Paulina, alone with Roberto after having sent Gerardo on an errand, threatens to shoot him. She demands: "The truth, Doctor. The truth and I'll let you go. Repent and I'll let you go" (44). Conflating truth with repentance, Paulina shows us the impossibility of closure following such deliberately inflicted trauma. And the play's resolution enacts—and respects—the unresolvable nature of the aftermath of horror. It remains with the questions it raises, rather than evasively—and falsely—resolving them for its characters and for its audience. At a concert where Schubert's *Death and the Maiden* is being played (music that Paulina's rapist played on tape while abusing her), the scene change is created by a giant mirror being lowered, covering the final encounter between Paulina and Roberto with her demand for truth/repentance and his refusal. The audience sees themselves reflected in the mirror, and in the next scene Paulina and Gerardo have taken their place with the audience, backs to the audience and facing the stage, also reflected in the mirror. We also see Roberto at the concert. (The stage directions say that he "could be real or he could be an illusion in Paulina's head.") And the curtain is lowered as the musicians play on.

In contrast, the film (of which Dorfman was a coproducer and coscreenwriter) fails to stay with the terrible truths of torture, witnessing, testimony, and the passage of time. Its overly resolved ending is evident from its beginning. The film begins where it ends (and where the play ended but didn't begin). The opening scene of the concert shows us the three protagonists, elegantly dressed and out for an evening's concert, an assurance of its "happy end" from the outset. This becomes clear to viewers midway through the film when the significance of Schubert's music to Paulina is revealed. The film turns the play into a thriller, with appropriate camera shots and musical emphases, culminating in Roberto's confession at the edge of a cliff. Paulina is pointing a gun and Gerardo listening while Roberto clarifies his deeds, describes how he was seduced by and attracted to torture and rape, thus repenting. The film takes care to ensure that the audience is left with no doubts. Roberto gives information that only Paulina and her rapist could know. She has told Gerardo/us that she was raped fourteen times; he confesses to having raped her fourteen times. It is clear that Roberto is not confessing to something that he did not do in order to save his life; it is clear that he is not fabricating a story under duress.

In his play, Dorfman exploits the heteroglossic potential of drama. He does not present his audience with a single mediated narrative. The play confronts viewers (through doubling with the character of Gerardo) with two seemingly opposed narratives and a need for judgment even within the doubt that is a component of all reflective political action. The film does the opposite. It retreats via a heavily mediating camera and thriller-genre music, resolving all doubt finally by a fully articulated confession that lets everyone off the hook. No one—character or audience—has to live with the shadow of a doubt that the play (and most real-life situations) ineluctably contains.

In his afterword to the version of the play that he published as the "final definitive edition" (or so the cover claims), Dorfman explains why he chose to present this material as a play rather than a novel. In the aftermath of a brutal dictatorship, he writes,

> many Chileans were asking themselves [questions] privately . . . [that] hardly anyone seemed interested in posing in public. How can those who tortured and those who were tortured co-exist in the same land? How to heal a country that has been traumatised by repression if the fear to speak out is still omnipresent everywhere? And how do you reach the truth if lying has become a habit? How do we keep the past alive without becoming its prisoner? How do we forget it without risking its repetition in the future? Is it legitimate to sacrifice the truth to ensure peace? And what are the consequences of suppressing that past and the truth it is whispering or howling to us? Are people free to search for justice and equality if the threat of a military intervention haunts them? And given these circumstances, can violence be avoided? And how guilty are we all of what happened to those who suffered most? And perhaps the greatest dilemma of them all: how to confront these issues without destroying the national consensus which creates democratic stability? (48–49)

These were the questions that generated *Death and the Maiden* for Dorfman in three weeks. His afterword expresses a belief in the power of his play to "be an instrument through which we explore our identity and the contradictory options available to us in the years to come," and rejects the assurance that "there is an easy, even facile, comforting answer to most of our problems" such as those promoted by "the mass entertainment media" (49). Distinguishing his play from such "mass entertainment" and its false solutions, Dorfman writes:

Such an aesthetic strategy seems to me not only to falsify and disdain human experience but in the case of Chile or any country that is coming out of a period of enormous conflict and pain, it turns out to be counterproductive for that community, freezing its maturity and growth. . . . *Death and the Maiden* . . . force[s] the spectators to confront those predicaments that, if not brought into the light of day, could lead to their ruin. (49)

An experience of "recognition" is what Dorfman wants to give his audience (50), that moment of grace granted the tragic hero that Dorfman now seeks for his audience, which is in a sense his tragic hero. That audience is described by the playwright as

that submerged zone of our species who live far from the centres of power but are often near the quick center of suffering where ethical choices determine the immediate shape of things to come and things to be postponed. . . . [I]t may help us a bit . . . to think of the Paulinas, the Gerardos, the Robertos, of the world—to figure out for ourselves which of these three we most resemble, how much of our secluded lives are expressed in each of these characters and in all of them. (50)

"Figuring out for ourselves" is an opportunity his play provides and his film precludes. Among the questions he describes as his lifelong obsessions, Dorfman asks: "How do we find a language that is political and not pamphletary? How to tell stories that are both popular and ambiguous . . . ?" (50). Perhaps one of the burdens—and sports—of life is the eschatological drive for clear resolution, for clear linkage of past to present (and thus, by implication, future), for the costly comfort of clarity as represented in illusory overresolution such as that of Dorfman's film and Schlink's novel, a facile resolution exquisitely challenged by Dorfman's play.[3]

Frank Kermode offers a useful distinction relevant to this reading of narrative resolution. Kermode distinguishes between myth and fiction (1966: 39–43), where fiction "inescapably involves an encounter with oneself." He elaborates the distinction thus: "Fictions are for finding things out, and they change as the needs of sense-making change. Myths are the agents of stability, fictions the agents of change. Myths call for absolute, fictions for conditional assent" (39). Warning against the seduction of myth, Kermode asserts that "we must avoid the regress into myth which has deceived poet, historian, and critic. Our satisfactions will be hard to find"

(43). These satisfactions are what Dorfman warns against in his afterword, the comforts offered by what he describes as "mass entertainment media"—comforts by which he himself is seduced in his screenplay.

The outlines of a more reflective writing begin to emerge in response to increased awareness of the ethical implications of writing and reading. Two salient features can be articulated thus far. Part II of this book contemplates realization of Seyla Benhabib's concepts of concrete and generalized others in narrative choices and its potential for writing metanarrative. This epilogue posits a narrative integrity between questions raised and resolutions offered as a basis for discussion of ethics and narrative. And this tentative ending of my own metanarrative is a political—and pedagogical—position, aiming to invite readers into my text by this self-reflexive fissure of irresolute ending, hoping to expand this conversation across disciplines, in directions unforeseen.

Notes

1. See Genette (1980 [1972]), Rimmon-Kenan (1989 [1983]), Rabinowitz (1987), Herman (1999).

2. See van Dijk (1976, 1993, 1997), Johnstone (2001).

3. See Mieke Bal's (2002) stimulating and generous conceptual, theoretical, personal, and professional account of this process.

4. This coinage is a species-variant of what Kenneth Burke calls a "terministic screen," used to direct and frame analytic attention (1966: 46–50).

5. McGee also categorizes elective and compulsory applications of this conceptualization according to textual selection. By working across periods and genres, I hope to demonstrate how compelling this conceptualization can be for contemporary and historically more distant texts.

6. In her essay on "The Rhetorical Limits of Polysemy," Condit notes that "responses and interpretations are generally polyvalent, and texts themselves are occasionally or partially polysemic" (1999: 498). Fissures are also conceptually useful here, both in mapping the polysemic limits of texts and in suggesting the range of polyvalent [audience/reader] response.

7. It is interesting too to note how invigorating this interdisciplinary tool-sharing is when returned to its sources. In their recent book, Catherine Gallagher and Stephen Greenblatt write of the way "that Geertz's account of the project of social science rebounded with force upon literary critics like us . . . made sense of something we were already doing, returning our own professional skills to us as more important, more vital and illuminating, than we had ourselves grasped" (2000:20).

8. See Foss (1996, 1999), McKerrow in (2001: 620); also Mailloux (1997: 379) on the relationship between rhetoric and hermeneutics.

9. See also Barker and Galasinski (2001: 25–27; 62–85).

10. See also Clifford Geertz (2000: 17): "kinship, village form, the traditional state, calendars, law, and, most infamously, the cockfight could be read as texts, or, to quiet the literal-minded, 'text-analogues'—enacted statements of, in another exposing phrase, particular ways of being in the world."

11. At this point, I would like to position myself briefly within my own metanarrative. Coming from the study of English literature to teaching rhetorical analysis in the Lafer Center for Gender Studies at the Hebrew University in Jerusalem, my work inevitably reflects my location(s), academic and geographic. Some of the texts I use to demonstrate the textual fissures that are the focus of this chapter are translated from the Hebrew-speaking culture within which I live and work.

12. In the short run, this strategy seems not to have helped. Ehud Barak won

that election. But perhaps time teaches a different lesson. The political liability clearly reflected in this slogan seems forgotten, and Benjamin Netanyahu seems to have reestablished his political base.

13. The move to the longer unit of narrative enables us to study fissures as a feature of discourse analysis. "What we find beyond the sentence is *discourse* in the proper sense of the word, that is, a sequence of sentences presenting their own rules of composition (taking charge of this ordered aspect of discourse was, for a long time, the heritage of classical rhetoric). The narrative is one of the largest classes of discourse, that is, of sequences of sentences subsumed to a certain order" (Ricoeur 1981: 281).

14. See Booth's description of his seminal study, *The Rhetoric of Fiction*, as a pursuit of "the author's means of controlling his reader" (1983: xiii). I prefer Foucault's image to Booth's for its emphasis on function, facilitating focus on what the text does, rather than what a certain historical personage might have been doing.

15. On the practical application of the study of writing for ethnographers, Clifford Geertz notes: "The advantage of shifting at least part of our attention from the fascinations of field work, which have held us so long in thrall, to those of writing is not only that this difficulty will become more clearly understood, but also that we shall learn to read with a more percipient eye" (1988: 24). Hence my qualification about the functionality of my division into separate spheres of reading and writing; their reciprocity is assumed.

16. See Booth (1989) for an interestingly skeptical consideration of this question.

NOTES TO PART I

1. I use the phrase "resisting reader" not in Judith Fetterley's sense of an actual reader's deliberate self-positioning, but rather as a function of the text and its narration; its implied reader.

2. In contrast, see Paul Ricoeur's agonistic author-reader model: "reading . . . is at its best a struggle between two strategies, the *strategy of seduction* pursued by the author in the guise of a more or less trustworthy narrator, with the complicity of the 'willing suspension of disbelief' (Coleridge) that marks the entry into reading, and the *strategy of suspicion* pursued by the vigilant reader, who is not unaware of the fact that she brings the text to meaningfulness thanks to its lacunae, whether these be intended or not" (1992: 159, note 23).

3. As Catherine Gallagher and Stephen Greenblatt explain,

> nineteenth-century fiction is the most highly developed genre of the probable, an explicitly fictional form that does not ask its readers to believe its characters actually existed or the events really took place, but instead invites us to appreciate the *believable* as such. . . . Novels may therefore be said to activate a fundamental practice of modern ideology— acquiescence without belief, crediting without credulousness—while significantly altering its disposition, transforming the usually guarded wariness into pleasurable expectations. Whether this transformation strengthens one's attachment to dynamics of domination or, obversely, establishes expectations of pleasure unrealizable in the social world; whether, in the latter case, those expectations prove in themselves engrossing enough to compen-

sate for the experience of social powerlessness or, instead, inspire resistance; whether fictional realism makes the ideological subject by providing those very experiences of resistance, or simply has no social or political effects whatsoever: these controversial issues are unresolvable by either literary theory or critical analysis. (2000: 169–70)

4. For a look at this type of ventriloquism in poetry, see Alan Michael Parker and Mark Wilhardt's 1996 anthology, *The Routledge Anthology of Cross-Gendered Verse*.

5. As Madeleine Kahn puts it in her study of eighteenth-century male-authored cross-gendered texts (a crossing she terms "narrative transvestism," using a psychoanalytic model), "the most incisive question we can pose about a male author's use of a female narrative voice is not, did he create a believable woman? but, what did he have to gain from the attempt? What is the point of creating a rather elaborate narrative structure to gain access to a voice on the other side of the structural divide between genders?" (1991: 10).

However, I disagree with her assertion that "the question, what does a woman author have to gain from using a man's voice? turns out not to be symmetrical to, what does a male author have to gain from using a woman's?" (2). Although Kahn goes on to note that "[w]omen are borrowing the voice of authority; men are seemingly abdicating it," her commitment to her metaphor of transvestism prevents her from seeing the symmetry of this "borrowing" and "abdicating." Elizabeth Harvey's study of cross-gendering in Renaissance literature coins a similar phrase in speaking of "transvestite ventriloquism," but offers a feminist (as opposed to Kahn's psychoanalytic) interpretation of narrative crossing as an exploitation of cultural power politics where "the issue is not epistemological at all, but ethical and political. It is not whether male poets <u>can</u> adequately represent the female voice, but the ethics and politics of doing so" (1992: 12, original emphasis). It is precisely this relationship of author to authority that both female and male authors exploit in gender-crossing, the female writer moving from margin to center and the male from center to margin.

6. As Joseph Boone writes, "the degree to which a fictional construct attempts to enclose its meanings and thereby create the appearance of a totalizing simulacrum of 'order' can be measured in terms of specific textual strategies and techniques, which in turn illuminate the writer's allegiances or infidelities to reigning narrative and social conventions" (1987: 146).

CHAPTER 1. ON PREFACING

1. In an interesting contemporary appropriation of Mary Shelley's text, Kenneth Branagh's film, prefaced by the claim of its title to tell "Mary Shelley's *Frankenstein*," adds original script to her text while claiming the authenticity of its adaptation in the possessive of its title. One very compelling addition relates to the protagonist's motivation. Branagh locates the motive for Victor Frankenstein's scientific explorations in his anguish over his mother's death in childbirth, which he witnesses (in the novel she dies of scarlet fever). Thus Branagh gives Shelley's

protagonist her biography (Mary Shelley's mother died giving birth to her) as he translates her novel into film.

In another contemporary appropriation of *Frankenstein*, Theodore Roszak rewrites the novel as *The Memoirs of Elizabeth Frankenstein* (1995), telling the story from the point of view of Victor Frankenstein's adopted sister and, later, fiancée. Roszak frames Elizabeth's diary with a preface and epilogue by Walton, Mary Shelley's frame narrator, and includes frequent "editor's notes," Walton's comments on the diary, including relevant fictional scholarship and fictional scientific research. Roszak's cross-gendering here is as much a reflection of his late-twentieth-century American culture as Mary Shelley's is of her early-nineteenth-century British culture. His Walton is a narrator whose sincerity and limitations are immediately and concomitantly displayed, creating reader resistance to his narrative and reader complicity with Elizabeth's. In an "author's note" introducing the novel, Roszak explains that he "had long felt that the *Frankenstein* Mary most wanted to offer the world lies hidden in the under-story that only Elizabeth could have written" (ix). In a concluding conflation of himself with both Elizabeth Frankenstein and Mary Shelley, Roszak expresses his "hope that, speaking here as the bride of Frankenstein, she [Mary Shelley] will at last find the voice she was not free to adopt in her own day." Ironically, this most recent male appropriation of *Frankenstein*, with its claims to amplify Mary Shelley's muted voice through reimagining her characters in a cross-gendered narrative, is a cliche-ridden fantasy of late-twentieth-century politically acceptable feminist Gothic. (Surprisingly sharing Roszak's view of his work as a corrective, Nina Auerbach, a contemporary feminist critic, declares that "[i]n *The Memoirs of Elizabeth Frankenstein*, Theodore Roszak corrects Mary Shelley by galvanizing her women into life" [*The New York Times Book Review*, 11 June 1995].)

Percy Shelley's 1817 appropriation spoke in the first-person as if he were Mary; Roszak's 1995 appropriation claims to speak "at last" as Mary would have wanted to. I believe, as I argue in this chapter, that it is at the heart of her novel, in the monster's narrative at its center, that Mary Shelley's voice is most clearly heard.

2. Mary Shelley's parents were Mary Wollstonecraft, early feminist and author of *A Vindication of the Rights of Woman* (1792) and William Godwin, philosopher and author (of essays and novels, among them *Things As They Are, or the Adventures of Caleb Williams*, 1794).

3. Walton's letters, which create the frame narrative of *Frankenstein*, span the nine months from "Dec. 11, 17__" to "September 12th." In an interpretive thread that I do not pursue here but that has informed many feminist readings of the novel, *Frankenstein* can be read as a birth myth written by a writer whose own birth was also the occasion of her mother's death. Birth can also be a metaphor for the creative process allegorized in the novel; Shelley refers to her scientist protagonist as "artist" in her introduction. Describing her novel's origin in a dream, she tells of how "[h]is success would terrify the <u>artist</u>" (10, my emphasis). See also note 5 below.

4. See the introductory chapter on Foucault and the author function.

5. For other readings of the story of *Frankenstein*, note especially Ellen Moer's reading of *Frankenstein* as a birth myth (1963), Sandra Gilbert and Susan Gubar's reading of *Frankenstein* as a rewriting of Milton's *Paradise Lost* (1979), Barbara Johnson's reading of *Frankenstein* as offering a theory of female autobiog-

raphy (1982), and Orit Kamir's reading of *Frankenstein* in a context of stalking narratives (2001).

6. For more on muted-group theory, see Ardener (1975).

7. See Mellor (1988) for an analysis of the original manuscript and the changes made by Percy Shelley. Particularly relevant to my reading is her note on Percy Shelley's introjection of the word "author" with reference to Frankenstein (Shelley: 86; Mellor: 65), causing critics to link Mary Shelley to Victor Frankenstein rather than to his monster, as in my reading of the novel.

Chapter 2. On Framing

1. *Frankenstein* has both prefatory and narrative framing; see the discussion of Walton in chapter 1.

2. Wolfgang Iser coins this term (1978: 34) on the ground laid by Wayne Booth's implied author (Booth 1983[1961]: 158–59). For both the point is to emphasize the readers and writers whom we discuss as <u>constructs</u> anchored in texts and not historical or real persons. For a survey of reader-response criticism, one of the critical approaches that evolved from this desire to discuss readers and writers in textual terms, see Freund, 1987.

3. Elizabeth Harvey makes an observation about what she terms "transvestite ventriloquism" in the Renaissance, which has interesting conjunctions with my reading of *Turn of the Screw*. Harvey observes that

> it becomes clear that there is a profound affinity between the representation of the abandoned woman and male constructions of the feminine voice. . . . Its ventriloquized status gives it a special force, since it seems to be spoken by its victim, but is almost always in the Renaissance the vehicle of a patriarchal didacticism, a way of controlling female desire and promulgating a particular version of female sexuality, one that relies on or responds to a forceful, sometimes violent male sexuality. Its passionately static nature, and its repetitive, often formulaic rhetoric depict a kind of cultural imprisonment of feminine erotic experience, and the very excesses of its expression seem confounded by the narrowness of experiential possibility. (1992: 140–41)

Chapter 4. On Temporary and Permanent Gaps

1. Shlomith Rimmon-Kenan defines these succinctly. Temporary gaps are "filled-in at some point in the text" and permanent gaps "remain open even after the text has come to an end" (1989: 128).

2. See the introduction on this aspect of narrative time. Duration of narrated events is measured by comparing textual length to chronological time represented.

Notes to Part II

1. On this problem of positioning and feminist methodology, see Jehlen (2001 [1981]).

2. For an extended meditation on this rhetorical move, see David Simpson (2002), *Situatedness, or Why We Keep Saying Where We're Coming From*.

3. I borrow the term and, I hope, the approach, from Elaine Showalter's description of Margaret Fuller's adult education classes, which Fuller called "conversations" (Showalter 2001: 47–48). This conversation is a cross-, inter-, and multidisciplinary exchange that has increasingly found voice(s) and form(s) in academic discourse, while failing, as yet, to significantly challenge traditional and normative academic disciplinary structures.

CHAPTER 5. AN EMERGENT GENRE

This chapter was written in response to Tamar El-Or's richly suggestive and challenging overview of the trend in anthropology to fieldwork in sites that she has labeled "zones of suffering" (El-Or, 2001).

1. See Bakhtin 1981, esp. pp. 324, 411.

2. See the epilogue on strategies of narrative resolution in relation to ethics.

CHAPTER 6. SPEAKING THE UNSPEAKABLE

1. For interesting early feminist readings of this story, see Simone de Beauvoir (1949) and Kate Millet (1968).

2. This is what Catharine MacKinnon critiques as "the neutral posture, . . . 'objectivity,' that is, the nonsituated distanced standpoint . . . the male standpoint, socially." She argues

> that the relationship between objectivity as the stance from which the world is known, and the world that is apprehended in this way, is the relationship of objectification. Objectivity is the epistemological stance of which objectification is the social process, of which male dominance is the politics, the acted out social practice; that is, to look at the world objectively is to objectify it. The act of control . . . is itself eroticized under male supremacy. . . . Gender here is a matter of dominance, not difference. (1988: 107)

3. See Part II on Seyla Benhabib's concepts of generalized and concrete others, and their relevance for questions of writing metanarratives.

4. On indeterminacy and reader activation, see Iser 1989: 28; and Iser 1978: 169, 189. On ethical implications of this choice, see also my epilogue.

5. My reading of Mew's choice of narrative mode is strongly opposed to that of Sandra Gilbert and Susan Gubar, who claim "that Mew chooses to relate the timeless nightmare of 'A White Night' from the point of view of a male narrator indicates the author's own belief that the male perspective on the spectacle of female sacrifice is a normative one, and that the female horror at such a spectacle is unspeakable" (1988: 84).

6. See also Kenneth Burke on Poe's poetics (1966: 26–27).

Epilogue

1. See also Burke (1966: 45–50).

2. I am reading overly resolved endings as a "strategy of containment" revealing a text's ideology. See Jameson (1981: 51–54).

3. In this regard, see the discussion in chapter 5 of Vincent Crapanzano's *Waiting* and its deliberate lack of resolution. His study of perpetrators and collaborators in apartheid subverts the possibility of resolution by compromising his speaking voice, implicating it in the inevitable corruption of living in a corrupt society.

Bibliography

Adams, Jon K. (1985). *Pragmatics and Fiction*. Amsterdam and Philadelphia: John Benjamins Publishing Co.

Ardener, Edwin. (1975). "The 'Problem' Revisited." In *Perceiving Women*. ed. Shirley Ardener. London: Malaby Press, pp. 19–27.

Bakhtin, M. M. (1981). *The Dialogic Imagination*. Edited by Michael Holquist. Translated by Caryl Emerson and Michael Holquist. Austin: University of Texas Press.

Bal, Mieke. (2002). *Travelling Concepts in the Humanities*. Toronto, Buffalo, and London: University of Toronto Press.

Barker, Chris, and Dariusz Galasinski (2001). *Cultural Studies and Discourse Analysis: A Dialogue on Language and Identity*. London: Sage Publications Ltd.

Barthes, Roland. (1985). "Day by Day with Roland Barthes." In *On Signs: A Semiotics Reader*. Edited by Marshall Blonsky. Oxford: Basil Blackwell, pp. 98–117.

Behar, Ruth. (1996). *The Vulnerable Observer*. Boston: Beacon Press.

Benhabib, Seyla. (1992). *Situating the Self: Gender, Community and Postmodernism in Contemporary Ethics*. Cambridge: Polity Press.

Bercovitch, Sacvan. (1996). "A Literary Approach to Cultural Studies." In *Fieldwork: Sites in Literary and Cultural Studies*. Edited by Marjorie Garber, Rebecca L. Walkowitz, Paul B. Franklin. London and New York: Routledge, pp. 247–55.

Boone, Joseph Allen. (1987). *Tradition Counter Tradition: Love and the Form of Fiction*. Chicago and London: University of Chicago Press.

Booth, Wayne. (1983) [1961]. *The Rhetoric of Fiction*. Chicago and London: University of Chicago Press.

———. (1989). "Are Narrative Choices Subject to Ethical Criticism?" In *Reading Narrative: Form, Ethics, Ideology*. Edited by James Phelan. Columbus: Ohio State University Press, pp. 57–78.

Bourdieu, Pierre. (1996). "Understanding." *Theory Culture and Society: Explorations in Critical Social Science* 13, no. 2, pp. 17–37.

———. (2000) [1977]. *Outline of a Theory of Practice*. Translated by Richard Nice. Cambridge: Cambridge University Press.

———. (2001). *Masculine Domination*. Translated by Richard Nice. Oxford: Polity Press.

Burke, Kenneth. (1966). *Language as Symbolic Action: Essays on Life, Literature, and Method*. Berkeley, Los Angeles, London: University of California Press.

Cameron, Deborah, ed. (1990). *The Feminist Critique of Language: A Reader*. New York and London: Routledge.

140

Chambers, Ross. (1984). *Story and Situation: Narrative Seduction and the Power of Fiction*. Minneapolis: University of Minnesota Press.

Clifford, James. (1986). "Introduction: Partial Truths." In *Writing Culture: The Poetics and Politics of Ethnography*. Berkeley: University of California Press, pp. 1–26.

Coetzee, J. M. (1990). *Age of Iron*. London: Penguin Books Ltd.

Condit, Celeste Michelle. (1999). "The Rhetorical Limits of Polysemy." In *Contemporary Rhetorical Theory: A Reader*. Edited by John Louis Lucaites, Celeste Michelle Condit, Sally Caudill. New York and London: The Guilford Press, pp. 494–511.

Crapanzano, Vincent. (1985). *Waiting: The Whites of South Africa*. New York: Random House.

Crawford, Mary and Roger Chaffin. (1986). "The Reader's Construction of Meaning: Cognitive Research on Gender and Comprehension." in *Gender and Reading: Essays on Readers, Texts, and Contexts*. Edited by Elizabeth Flynn and Patrocinio P. Schweickart. Baltimore: The Johns Hopkins University Press, pp. 3–30.

de Beauvoir, Simone. (1961) [1949]. *The Second Sex*. Translated by H. M. Parshley. New York: Bantam Books.

de Certeau, Michel. (1984). *The Practice of Everyday Life*. Translated by Steven Rendall. Berkeley, Los Angeles, London: University of California Press.

Defoe, Daniel. (1959) [1722]. *Moll Flanders*. Boston: Houghton Mifflin Co., Riverside Editions.

Dorfman, Ariel. (1994) [1991]. *Death and the Maiden*. London: Nick Hern Books. *Death and the Maiden* (1994), film directed by Roman Polanski.

Dorris, Michael. (1987). *A Yellow Raft in Blue Water*. New York: Warner Books, Inc.

El-Or, Tamar. (2001). "Anthropology of Zones of Suffering." The Hebrew University of Jerusalem, Dept. of Sociology and Anthropology (unpublished manuscript).

Felman, Shoshana. (1993). *What Does a Woman Want? Reading and Sexual Difference*. Baltimore and London: Johns Hopkins University Press.

Fetterley, Judith. (1978). *The Resisting Reader*. Bloomington: Indiana University Press.

Fisher, Walter R. (1987). *Human Communication as Narration: Toward A Philosophy of Reason, Value, and Action*. Columbia: University of South Carolina Press.

Foss, Sonja K. (1996). *Rhetorical Criticism: Exploration and Practice*. Prospect Heights, Ill.: Waveland Press, Inc.

Foss, Sonja K., Karen A. Foss, and Cindy L. Griffin. (1999). *Feminist Rhetorical Theories*. Thousand Oaks, Calif.: Sage Publications.

Foucault, Michel. (1980). "What Is an Author?" in *Language, Counter-Memory, Practice*. Edited by Donald Bouchard. Ithaca: Cornell University Press, pp. 196–210.

Fowler, Bridget. (1981). *Literature as Social Discourse: The Practice of Linguistic*

Criticism. Bloomington: Indiana University Press, and London: Batsford Academic and Educational Ltd.

———. (1996). "An Introduction to Pierre Bourdieu's 'Understanding.'" *Theory Culture and Society: Explorations in Critical Social Science* 13, no. 2, pp. 1–16.

Fowler, Roger. (1996). "On Critical Linguistics." In *Texts and Practices: Readings in Critical Discourse Analysis.* Carmen Rosa Caldas-Coulthard and Malcom Coulthard, eds. London: Routledge, pp. 3–14.

Frazer, Sir James George. (1980)[1922]. *The Golden Bough: A Study on Magic and Religion,* abridged edition. London: Macmillan Press Ltd.

Freund, Elizabeth. (1987). *The Return of the Reader: Reader-Response Criticism.* London and New York: Methuen.

Furman, Nelly. (1980). "Textual Feminism." In *Women and Language in Literature and Society.* Edited by Sally McConnell-Ginet, Ruth Borker, Nelly Furman. New York: Praeger Publishers. pp. 45–54.

Gallagher, Catherine, and Stephen Greenblatt. (2000). *Practicing New Historicism.* Chicago and London: University of Chicago Press.

Geertz, Clifford. (1973). *The Interpretation of Cultures.* New York: Basic Books.

———. (1988). *Works and Lives: The Anthropologist as Author.* Stanford: Stanford University Press.

———. (1995). *After the Fact: Two Countries, Four Decades, One Anthropologist.* Cambridge: Harvard University Press.

———. (2000). *Available Light; Anthropological Reflections on Philosophical Topics.* Princeton: Princeton University Press.

Genette, Gerard. (1980) [1972]. *Narrative Discourse: An Essay in Method.* Translated by Jane E. Lewin. Ithaca: Cornell University Press.

Gilbert, Sandra M., and Susan Gubar. (1988). *No Man's Land: The Place of the Woman Writer in the Twentieth Century. Vol. I: The War of the Words.* New Haven: Yale University Press.

Girard, Rene. (1977) [1972]. *Violence and the Sacred.* Translated by Patrick Gregory. Baltimore and London: Johns Hopkins University Press.

Godwin, William. (1982) [1794]. *Caleb Williams.* Oxford: Oxford University Press.

Goffman, Erving. (1970) [1963]. *Stigma: Notes on the Management of Spoiled Identity.* Harmondsworth, England: Penguin Books Ltd.

Gordimer, Nadine. (1990). *My Son's Story.* Harmondsworth, England: Penguin Books Ltd.

Greenberg, Joseph. (1966). *Language Universals.* The Hague: Mouton and Co.

Hartmann, Heidi. (1981). "The Unhappy Marriage of Marxism and Feminism: Towards a More Progressive Union." In *Women and Revolution: the Unhappy Marriage of Marxism and Feminism.* Edited by Lydia Sargent. London: Pluto Press.

Harvey, Elizabeth D. (1992). *Ventriloquized Voices; Feminist Theory and English Renaissance Texts.* London and New York: Routledge.

Helman, Sara, and Tamar Rapoport. (1997). "'These Are Ashkenazi Women, Single, Arafat's Sluts, Don't Believe in God and Don't Love the Land of Israel': 'Women in Black' and Challenging the Social Order." In Hebrew. *Teoria viBikoret [Theory and Criticism]* 10, 175–92.

Herman, David. (1999). "Toward a Socionarratology: New Ways of Analyzing Natural-Language Narratives." In *Narratologies: New Perspectives on Narrative Analysis*. ed. David Herman. Columbus: Ohio State University Press, pp. 218–46.

Hodge, Robert. (1990). *Literature as Discourse: Textual Strategies in English and History*. Cambridge: Polity Press.

Iser, Wolfgang. (1978). *The Act of Reading: A Theory of Aesthetic Response*. Baltimore and London: Johns Hopkins University Press.

———. (1989). *Prospecting; from Reader Response to Literary Anthropology*. Baltimore and London: Johns Hopkins University Press.

———. (1993). *The Fictive and the Imaginary; Charting Literary Anthropology*. Baltimore and London: Johns Hopkins University Press.

James, Henry. (1966) [1886]. *The Bostonians*. Harmondsworth, England: Penguin Books Ltd.

———. (1986) [1898]. *Turn of the Screw*. London: Penguin Books.

Jameson, Fredric. (1981). *The Political Unconscious: Narrative as a Socially Symbolic Act*. Ithaca: Cornell University Press.

Jehlin, Myra. (1981). "Archimedes and the Paradox of Feminist Criticism." *Signs: Journal of Women in Culture and Society* 6, pp. 575–601. Reprinted in Myra Jehlin. (2002). *Readings at the Edge of Literature*. Chicago and London: University of Chicago Press.

Johnson, Barbara. (1982). "My Monster/My Self." *Diacritics* 12, pp. 2–10.

Johnstone, Barbara. (2001). "Discourse Analysis and Narrative." In *The Handbook of Discourse Analysis*. Edited by Deborah Schiffrin, Deborah Tannen and Heidi E. Hamilton. Oxford: Blackwell Publishing, pp. 635–49.

Kahn, Madeleine. (1991). *Narrative Transvestism: Rhetoric and Gender in the Eighteenth-Century English Novel*. Ithaca and London: Cornell University Press.

Kamir, Orit. (2001). *Every Breath You Take; Stalking Narratives and the Law*. Ann Arbor: University of Michigan Press.

Kermode, Frank. (1966). *The Sense of an Ending: Studies in the Theory of Fiction*. Oxford: Oxford University Press.

Kleinman, Arthur. (1995). *Writing at the Margin: Discourse Between Anthropology and Medicine*. Berkeley: University of California Press.

———. (1999). "Moral Experience and Ethical Reflection: Can Ethnography Reconcile Them? A Quandry for 'The New Bioethics.' in *Daedalus* 128 (4), pp. 69–97.

Lawrence, D. H. (1934) [1928]. "The Woman Who Rode Away." In *The Tales of D. H. Lawrence*. London: William Heinemann Ltd., pp. 756–88.

Lear, Jonathan. (1990). *Love and Its Place in Nature: A Philosophical Interpretation of Freudian Psychoanalysis*. New York: Farrar, Straus and Giroux.

Liebes, Tamar, and Roni Grisek. (1993). "'Nurses Were Once Genuinely Merciful'—Television News and the Process of Politicization of Women in Israel." In Hebrew. *Zmanim 46–47*, 188–99.

Macherey, Pierre. (1978). *A Theory of Literary Production*. Translated by Geoffrey Wall. London: Routledge and Kegan Paul.

MacKay, Donald, and David Fulkerson. (1979). "On the Comprehension and Production of Pronouns." *Journal of Verbal Learning and Behavior* 18, 661–71.

MacKinnon, Catherine A. (1988). "Desire and Power: A Feminist Perspective." In *Marxism and the Interpretation of Culture*. Edited by Cary Nelson and Lawrence Grossberg. London: MacMillan Education Ltd.

Mailloux, Steven. (1997). "Articulation and Understanding: The Pragmatic Intimacy Between Rhetoric and Hermeneutics." In *Rhetoric and Hermenutics in Our Time: A Reader*. Edited by Walter Jost and Michael J. Hyde. New Haven and London: Yale University Press, pp. 378–394.

Matthiessen, F. O., and Kenneth B. Murdock, eds. (1961). *The Notebooks of Henry James*. New York: Oxford University Press.

McGee, Michael Calvin. (1999). "Text, Context, and the Fragmentation of Contemporary Culture." In *Contemporary Rhetorical Theory: A Reader*. Edited by John Louis Lucaites, Celeste Michelle Condit, Sally Caudill. New York and London: Guilford Press, pp. 65–78.

McKerrow, Raymie E. (1999). "Critical Rhetoric: Theory and Praxis." In *Contemporary Rhetorical Theory: A Reader*. Edited by John Louis Lucaites, Celeste, Michelle Condit, Sally Caudill. New York and London: Guilford Press, pp. 441–463.

———. (2001). "Critical Rhetoric." In *Encyclopedia of Rhetoric*. Edited by Thomas O. Sloane. New York: Oxford University Press, pp. 619–22.

Mellor, Anne K. (1988). *Mary Shelley: Her Life Her Fiction Her Monsters*. New York and London: Routledge, Chapman and Hall, Inc.

Mew, Charlotte. (1981) [1903]. "A White Night." In *Charlotte Mew: Collected Poems and Prose*. Edited by Val Warner. Manchester: Carcanet Press, in association with Virago Press.

Millett, Kate. (1970). *Sexual Politics*. New York: Ballantine Books.

Moer, Ellen. (1980) [1963]. *Literary Women*. London: Women's Press.

Morris, David B. (1997). "About Suffering: Voice, Genre, and Moral Community." In *Social Suffering*. Edited by Arthur Kleinman, Veena Das and Margaret Lock. Berkeley: University of California Press, pp. 24–45.

Ohmann, Richard. (1973). "Literature as Act." In *Approaches to Poetics: Selected Papers from the English Institute*. Edited by Seymour Chatman. New York: Columbia University Press, pp. 81–107.

Ong, Walter J. (1982). *Orality and Literacy; The Technologizing of the Word*. London: Routledge.

Parker, Alan Michael, and Mark Willhardt. (1996). *The Routledge Anthology of Cross-Gendered Verse*. London and New York: Routledge.

Poe, Edgar Allan. (1956) [1845]. *Selected Writings of Edgar Allan Poe*. Edited by Edward H. Davidson. Boston: Riverside Press.

Poulet, Georges. (1969). "Phenomenology of Reading." *New Literary History* 1, pp. 53–68.

Pratt, Mary Louise. (1986). "Fieldwork in Common Places." In *The Poetics and Politics of Ethnography*. Edited by James Clifford and George E. Marcus. Berkeley: University of California Press, pp. 27–50.

Price, Reynolds. (1986). *Kate Vaiden*. New York: Ballantine Books.

———. (1989). *A Common Room; Essays 1954–1987*. New York: Atheneum.

Rabinowitz, Peter. (1987). *Before Reading: Narrative Conventions and the Politics of Interpretation*. Ithaca and London: Cornell University Press.

Richards, I. A. (1965). *The Philosophy of Rhetoric*. New York: Oxford University Press.

Ricoeur, Paul. (1981). *Hermeneutics and the Human Sciences*. Edited and translated by John B. Thompson. Cambridge: Cambridge University Press.

———. (1984). *Time and Narrative*. Vol. 3. Translated by Kathleen McLaughlin and David Pellauer. Chicago and London: University of Chicago Press.

———. (1992). *Oneself as Another*. Translated by Kathleen Blamey. Chicago and London: University of Chicago Press.

Rimmon-Kenan, Shlomith. (1989) [1983]. *Narrative Fiction: Contemporary Poetics*. London and New York: Routledge.

Rosaldo, Renato. (1989). *Culture and Truth: The Remaking of Social Analysis*. Boston: Beacon Press.

Rosenthal, Gabriele. (1993). "Reconstruction of Life Stories: Principles of Selection in Generating Stories for Narrative Biographical Interviews." In *The Narrative Study of Lives*. Edited by Ruthellen Josselson and Amia Lieblich. Vol. 1. London: Sage.

Roszak, Theodore. (1995). *The Memoirs of Elizabeth Frankenstein*. New York: Random House.

Scheper-Hughes, Nancy. (1992). *Death Without Weeping: The Violence of Everyday Life in Brazil*. Berkeley: University of California Press.

———. (2000). "Ire in Ireland." in *Ethnography* 1(1), 117–40.

Schlink, Bernhard. (1997) [1995]. *The Reader*. Translated by Carol Brown Janeway. New York: Vintage Books.

Searle, John. (1968). *Speech Acts: An Essay in the Philosophy of Language*. Cambridge: Cambridge University Press.

———. (1975). "A Taxonomy of Illocutionary Acts." In *Language, Mind and Knowledge*. Edited by K. Gunderson. Minneapolis: University of Minnesota Press, pp. 344–69.

Sedgwick, Eve Kosofsky. (1990). *Epistemology of the Closet*. London: Harvester Wheatsheaf.

Shelley, Mary. (1961) [1817]. *Frankenstein; or the Modern Prometheus*. New York: Macmillan Publishing Co.

Showalter, Elaine. (1987) [1985]. *The Female Malady: Women, Madness and English Culture, 1830–1980*. London: Virago Press Ltd.

———. (2001). *Inventing Herself: Claiming a Feminist Intellectual Heritage*. London: Picador.

Silveira, Jeanette. (1980). "Generic Masculine Words and Thinking." In *The Voices and Words of Women and Men*. Edited by Chris Kramarae. Oxford and New York: Pergamon Press Ltd., pp. 165–78.

Simpson, David. (2002). *Situatedness, or Why We Keep Saying Where We're Coming From*. Durham, N.C., and London: Duke University Press.

Smith-Rosenberg, Carroll. (1972). "The Hysterical Woman: Sex Roles and Role Conflict in Nineteenth-Century America." *Social Research* 39, pp. 652–78.

Thompson, John B. (1984). *Studies in the Theory of Ideology*. Berkeley: University of California Press.

Turner, Mark. (1996). *The Literary Mind; The Origins of Thought and Language*. New York: Oxford University Press.

van Dijk, Teun A. (1976). "Pragmatics and Poetics." In *Pragmatics of Language and Literature*. Edited by Teun A. van Dijk. Amsterdam: North-Holland Publishing Co.

———. (1993). "Principles of Critical Discourse Analysis." *Discourse and Society* 4 249–83.

———. (1997). *Discourse Studies: A Multidisciplinary Introduction*. London: Sage Publications.

Veeder, William. (1986). *Mary Shelley and Frankenstein: The Fate of Androgyny*. Chicago and London: University of Chicago Press.

Watt, Ian. (1974) [1957]. *The Rise of the Novel*. Harmondsworth, England: Penguin.

Willis, Paul, and Mats Trondman. (2000). "Manifesto for *Ethnography*." In *Ethnography* 1(1), 5–16.

Woolf, Virginia. (1957) [1929]. *A Room of One's Own*. New York and London: Harcourt Brace Jovanovich.

Yacobi, Tamar. (1981). "Fictional Reliability as a Communicative Problem." *Poetics Today* 2, 113–26.

Index